MELBOURNE CUP 1930

MELBOURNE CUP 1930

How Phar Lap won Australia's greatest race

GEOFF ARMSTRONG AND
PETER THOMPSON

ALLEN&UNWIN

Endpaper photograph: La Trobe Picture Collection, State Library of Victoria

First published in 2005

Allen & Unwin
83 Alexander Street
Crows Nest NSW 2065
Australia
Phone: (61 2) 8425 0100
Fax: (61 2) 9906 2218
Email: info@allenandunwin.com
Web: www.allenandunwin.com

National Library of Australia
Cataloguing-in-Publication entry:
Armstrong, Geoff, 1961- .
    Melbourne Cup 1930: how Phar Lap won Australia's greatest race.

    ISBN 1 74114 750 6.

    1. Melbourne Cup (Horse race). 2. Horse racing - Victoria -
Melbourne - History. 3. Phar Lap (Race horse). 4. Race
horses - Australia. I. Thompson, Peter, 1960- . II. Title.

798.40099451

Text design and typesetting by Kirby Jones
Printed in Australia by McPherson's Printing Group

10 9 8 7 6 5 4 3 2 1

CONTENTS

Weights and Measures

Foot: A foot is an Imperial measure of length, equalling 12 inches or 30.48 centimetres.

Furlong: A furlong is 220 yards (one eighth of a mile). When racecourses in Australia began to use metric measures (on August 1, 1972), a furlong was approximated to 200 metres (in fact it is 201.168 metres).

Guinea: A British gold coin of the value of 21 shillings. The coin was taken out of circulation in 1813, but the term was retained.

Hands: A horse's height is measured in hands, one hand equalling four inches. This height is the vertical distance from the middle of the horse's withers (the lumpy bit where the neck joins the back) to the ground. Most thoroughbreds are between 15 and 17 hands tall.

Length: Winning margins and the margins between placegetters are measured in lengths. A length is the distance from the winning horse's nose to the back of its hindquarters.

Mile: A mile is 1760 yards, eight furlongs, or 1609 metres.

Pound (lb): A measure of weight. An avoirdupois pound is divided into 16 ounces. A pound is equivalent to 0.454kg; 1kg is equivalent to 2.203lb.

Pound (£): A monetary unit in Australia until 1966. A colloquial term for a pound was a 'quid'.

Shillings and Pennies: Other monetary units of Phar Lap's day — there were 12 pennies in a shilling and 20 shillings in a pound. A shilling was also known as a 'bob'.

Sixpence: A silver coin worth six pennies, sometimes known as a 'zac'.

Stone: A measure of weight equivalent to 14lb or 6.356kg. Until 1972, weight as carried by horses was expressed in stones and pounds.

Two Miles: The traditional race distance of the Melbourne Cup. Since 1972, the Cup has been run over 3200 metres, which is approximately 61 and a half feet shorter than two miles.

Yard: A yard is three feet, or 0.9144 metres.

Weight: Whether the race be a handicap or run at 'set weights', a horse is required to carry the weight allotted to it. The jockey, his helmet, his whip and his saddle make up this weight. Thus, when jockeys are struggling to get down to a horse's allocation they use as light a saddle as possible. If the jockey is light and requires extra to make up the designated weight, thin pieces of lead are added to bags under the saddle.

PREFACE

By the end of October 1930, Australia was gripped by 'Phar Lap fever'. A big chestnut gelding who stood an imposing 17.1 hands and who at full speed galloped with an enormous stride, Phar Lap had paralysed betting on the country's most famous horse race, the Melbourne Cup. His name came from the Siamese word for 'lightning'. Day after day, he was the lead story in the racing pages. His trainer said that the only way the horse could lose was if he was killed. The menacing phone calls the trainer was receiving and the ugly rumours he was hearing were threatening exactly that.

Who was the source of this intimidation? Broad coalitions of people have been vilified, guilt has been assumed, myth has become legend. Studies of newspaper reports of the day, of dependable and unreliable eyewitness accounts, and of official police files offer clues as to the identity of the perpetrators of this tale's most dastardly act, but no certainty.

The twin objectives of this book are to bring a fantastic story back to life and to sift through the fact and fiction to get as close as possible to the truth of the matter. All the characters in this book, human and equine, were really there for the 1930 Cup, except for one bookmaker, who has been created so no innocent party might be incriminated.

For Phar Lap, getting to the barrier would be an achievement in itself. To win, he would have to prove he was as great a galloper as the nation had ever seen. There have been many remarkable Melbourne Cups, but never one as extraordinary as this ...

CHAPTER ONE

ONE HELL OF A STORY

TOMMY WOODCOCK WAS SCARED. The whispers had been around all week, but at the track this morning they'd been more like a roar. Your horse'll be poisoned, he was told, or shot, run over, bombed. It'll happen today, tomorrow, maybe even during the running of the Melbourne Cup itself. Be careful, son, be very careful. For the past two weeks, Woodcock's boss, trainer Harry Telford, had been getting ugly phone calls along the same lines, and there'd been rumours about for months of a doping gang operating on Melbourne's racetracks.

So now, as the young horseman sat on a white pony leading his thoroughbred out of Caulfield racecourse and into a city he hardly knew, there was someone behind every fence. Every noise was a footstep, every shadow a gangster.

Woodcock was in Melbourne for the racing festival all Australia knew as the 'spring carnival'. This was the dawn of Derby Day, the Saturday before the Cup. It was hardly chilly, but this early in the morning of the first day of November the flared nostrils of a horse could still spit steam into the air. These were sights and sounds that Woodcock had grown up with and he loved them. In many ways where he found himself was glorious — walking the Cup favourite as the sky began to come to life, the air fresh, the day new, the figures on the track and in the on-course stable areas not so much ghostly as grey. But the stories on the track and the crank calls to Mr Telford nagged mightily at him. The poor man's mind was racing.

He looked up both sides of Manchester Grove, the street that ran from the back of the course up to Glenhuntly Road, and could make out a variety of houses on either side, market gardens, the odd stable, empty lots. A generation earlier, this was the city's fringe; even now, it was not quite fully suburbia. Suddenly, a dog barked, and he felt like he jumped a mile.

Manchester Grove was not the usual way back to Joe Cripps' stables, but Mr Telford had ordered a change of routine, which seemed like a good idea. There were some cars owned by racing people parked around the track entrance, then nothing for all of two furlongs until, up near the picture theatre on Glenhuntly Road, a vehicle was sitting out of place, all on its own. Had the morning been any darker, he mightn't have seen it, but from this distance through the dawn he could make out enough to see it was flash and to believe it belonged to Al Capone himself.

Over the previous year and a bit, Woodcock and his galloper had become as close as any pair in racing history. The horse's stable name was 'Bobby' and Woodcock went everywhere with him. Back home in Sydney, when the two exercised around the streets of Kensington, near the famous Randwick racecourse, the locals often joked that it was the horse who took his strapper for a walk, rather than the other way round. But they were wrong. Woodcock's thin build and almost angelic features belied a toughness that only came to light when he was asked to calm a headstrong racehorse. Now he held the reins as tight as he could and didn't yell at the big chestnut, he whispered.

'Whoa Bobby, settle. Easy, Bobby. Easy.'

It's amazing what your brain can do to you in the space of 400 yards. When Woodcock took Bobby out onto Manchester Grove, after the initial trepidation he was nearly able to convince himself that the car was just a classy vehicle parked in a spot where you wouldn't usually see one at 10 to six in the morning. But with every crack of his horse's hooves on the hard dirt road the situation grew more sinister. A furlong to go, Woodcock saw that there were two men in the car. Bizarrely, both were on the driver's side. One in the front, one in the back. Each man seemed to be reading a newspaper, but if that's what they were really doing, they were both very shortsighted. Woodcock searched for reinforcements. Back near the entrance to the track, one of the local trainers was urging his horses to behave. Maybe he should wait, or loiter, or call out, but to do so would be a sign of weakness — for every pessimist who'd said those bloody threats were real, there'd been five larrikins who laughed that he was just another shirker from Sydney. He pressed on.

Too quickly, Woodcock drew just about level with the back of the car. A new Studebaker, blue, maybe green. The back number plate was scribbled in chalk. Woodcock thought it read '1556', and felt as if he'd signed his own death warrant simply by trying to memorise it. The sound of the engine firing at that very second sent another, starker chill up the young strapper's spine. The sideways glance he risked as he passed the car made matters even worse. The bloke in the back seat pulled his newspaper closer, masking his face. The man in the front had what might have been a handkerchief

3

over his nose, across his mouth. This was something straight out of a Chicago gangster movie. Only this was real.

Woodcock barely stopped to look for traffic. On the southern side of Glenhuntly Road, Manchester Grove becomes James Street, and three streets down James Street is Beverley Street, where he had to go but was too far away. He settled on a plan. Not a good one, he knew, but a plan nonetheless. 'C'mon, Bobby,' he called, 'get o'er here.' He tugged as hard as he dared, and convinced his mate to turn into Etna Street, first on the right, 75 yards south of Glenhuntly Road. Out of sight, he tried to open the gate into the backyard of the house on the corner, but it was locked shut. He looked across for a saviour, at least an ally, but saw only a paperboy, about the same height and build as himself but 10 or 12 years younger, cheerfully dragging his trolley along the other side of the street. The terror in Woodcock's eyes was enough, and the paperboy lost his smile and froze. Then they heard the screech of tyres as the Studebaker's engine roared, horn blaring as it bounced across the main road. Woodcock knew it was coming for him. All he could do was put Bobby between himself on his pony and the fence of the property he had just tried to enter. There was no point running. He was only 10 yards up Etna Street, a sitting duck.

The Studebaker cut the corner as it bounced too quickly into Etna Street, and hardly slowed as it drew level with Woodcock. To his horror, the strapper saw that the man in the back now had in his hands not a newspaper but a double-barrelled shotgun, aimed straight at him. The gunman hesitated, perhaps hoping for a better angle, but then Bobby, frightened by the commotion, reared and twisted 180 degrees, stumbling back slightly so his hindquarters were exposed. Woodcock saw the danger and bravely dug his heels into the pony's ribs, trying vainly to protect the big horse, but the pony jumped up rather than forward. The car was now maybe 20 yards away and on the paperboy's side of the street when the shotgun exploded. Only once, but from that distance surely enough. The pony broke away, terrified, while Woodcock hung onto Bobby's reins for grim death. The would-be assassins, meanwhile, were careering away, not brave or bothered enough to reflect on their crime, turning wildly right into Augusta Street, heading back towards Glenhuntly Road. They were hardly clinical. A few residents, roused by the mayhem, might have seen them go.

Woodcock scarcely knew what had happened. 'Whoa Bobby, whoa Bobby, whoa Bobby,' he spluttered over and over. He was angry, scared and relieved, mostly angry, and as soon as he dared he started checking out the legs, the hindquarters, the rump. The horse seemed fine. By now, perhaps a dozen people had gathered, and Woodcock kept muttering, 'He's all right, he's all right,' as he kept being asked, 'Is he okay? Is he okay?' He continued to brush his hand over the horse's hide, checking his joints, stroking his neck, seeking a wound that didn't exist, as if he was searching for a speck of dust on a billiards table. As soon as he saw a face he recognised, one of the boys from Cripps' stable, he asked quietly, 'Can you please go to the course and tell Mr Telford?'

The milkman, doing his rounds, had come across the pony and brought him back, as the crowd continued to build. A couple of blokes were already scouring the footpath for souvenirs, and by the way the people were talking and pointing, re-describing the atrocity as soon as anyone new arrived, Woodcock knew this was going to be one hell of a story. All he really wanted was to get home, so he dusted himself down, politely thanked all those who'd helped him, hopped back on the pony and the three of them were on their way. Only now did it occur to him that he'd been lucky.

No sooner was he out of sight, safe at last, and a newspaper reporter was on the scene. Notepad and pen at the ready, the 'journo' looked around for likely suspects. 'Did anyone see what happened?' he asked hopefully. Someone pointed at the paperboy.

At this stage, no one had thought to call the police.

ON A RACECOURSE, THE one thing that travels faster than the horses is information. The scene at the corner of James and Etna might have been chaotic, and Woodcock might have not long asked someone to go and fetch his employer, but back at the track, the mood was serene. But not for much longer. The sun was peeping over the horizon; it seemed like it was going to be a beautiful Derby Day.

Harry Telford was talking to his 16-year-old apprentice Bobby Parker, who'd just run the two-year-old filly Old Ming over five furlongs. Telford was a short, craggy-faced man with greying hair slicked back beneath a frayed old woollen cap, who looked every one of his 54 years. Some reckoned he was a difficult bloke, but he preferred to think he was simply reserved and told it as it was. He was all about loyalty — to its wife, his young son, those who worked for him and helped him, and most of all to his horses, the last of which had just finished its work, so now it was time to get back to Joe Cripps' place. Telford had been in the racing game in some shape or form for all his life, been a 'battling' trainer in Sydney for the best part of a decade, until suddenly last year he found the one in a hundred million, a big chestnut horse who won the Sydney and Melbourne Derbies, started favourite in the Cup and even provoked comparisons with the immortal Carbine. This had been very exciting and very profitable, thank you, until it all went skewiff in just the last couple of weeks. For Harry

Telford, the first Tuesday in November, the day they ran the Melbourne Cup, couldn't come quick enough.

It'd started a couple of Mondays ago when he scratched his champion from the Caulfield Cup. It wasn't the fact that he withdrew the horse that ignited the furore, but that he left it to the very last minute, causing — so the damn papers said — the ruination of Caulfield Cup–Melbourne Cup doubles betting. Telford had his own reasons for doing what he did, and they mightn't have been what the reporters were writing, but he didn't really give a hoot what anyone else thought. Then, though, the bloody phone calls started. What he had to do was get through today, make it to Tuesday, and maybe everything would be all right.

Parker had nothing else to say, the mare's work was good not great. So Telford gathered up his thoughts and things, and was ready to head home. Then he sensed something was wrong, and looked up to see a young apprentice jockey riding like the Man from Snowy River, urging his horse as fast as he dared up into a collection of trainers, stablehands and jockeys mingling near the centre of the course. 'He knows he shouldn't do that,' one old trainer grizzled, but the desperate look on the young bloke's face reflected the urgency of his mission. Telford was maybe 20 yards away. He hushed those around him, keen to hear what could possibly have happened. But the apprentice didn't whisper, he shouted the news the whole world was about to hear:

'Phar Lap's been shot!'

Harry Telford started running faster than he'd ever run in his life.

CHAPTER TWO

IT'S THE BOOKIES, MATE

HARRY TELFORD DIDN'T CONTACT the police until 8am. By then the local constabulary were aware of the incident because the press had quickly informed them about it, but until they received a complaint from the aggrieved party they couldn't really do much. Truth be told, Telford didn't want to involve the cops at all, but eventually he realised he had to, because he needed them to help get Phar Lap to the track in the afternoon. So he got it over with.

Ten minutes later, when Senior Constable Davis from Glenhuntly Police Station arrived at Joe Cripps' place he didn't exactly get the reception he was looking for. Mr Cripps' greeting was polite enough, but Telford and Woodcock didn't want to talk, while a third man, a short, squat individual dressed in a nice suit and wearing thick glasses, wanted to be noticed. This was David Davis, who introduced himself as an 'owner'. He was keen to post a reward. Now.

'Yes, Mr Davis, we can get to that,' said Senior Constable Davis. 'But first I'd like to talk to the lad.'

The 'lad', of course, was Woodcock. As they sat around the kitchen table, the strapper mumbled his name; when asked to repeat it, he mumbled it once more. Consequently, a couple of hours later, when one of the detectives assigned to the case asked Senior Constable Davis for Woodcock's first name, the young officer replied 'Trevor', and this was duly repeated in many of the papers that never actually got round to interviewing Tommy himself.

For the record, he was Aaron Treve Woodcock, but known to all as 'Tommy'. Senior Constable Davis realised that Woodcock was pretty shaken, but he also quickly concluded that the strapper had been briefed to say as little as possible, as if the incident was none of the police's business. However, slowly, he discovered something like the whole story, from leaving the course to getting back to Beverley Street. No, Woodcock didn't get a good view of their faces, because of the newspapers and because he didn't want to look too closely at them.

'Why not?' asked Senior Constable Davis.

'Because it wasn't right. Just looking at them, I thought to myself, it's on this morning,' Woodcock replied.

'What do you mean, "It's on"?'

Woodcock looked at Telford, who might have shaken his head. Something had been said that shouldn't have been said.

'Aw,' Woodcock hesitated. 'Mr Telford, he's been getting some letters and phone calls. That's why I used James Street to get to the track this morning, not Augusta Street like I had been. That's why he got me a pony. I can get home quicker on a pony than what I can running with him.'

'What kind of letters?'

After a pause, Telford spoke up. 'I've got a couple of letters and a few phone calls. People saying they're gonna shoot the horse.'

'Did you report them?' asked the policeman.

'No, I didn't.' The way Telford said it, Senior Constable Davis thought it best to move on. Davis knew that the detectives assigned to the case would be on the scene quick smart. If they wanted to pursue the matter, they were welcome.

'Mr Woodcock, can you describe the men in the car?'

'I dunno. Bloke in the back might've been 30.'

'Clean shaven?'

'Yeah.'

'Thin or fat?'

'Thin, I suppose.'

'Fair or dark complexion?

'Dark, maybe. Hard to tell.'

'And the driver?'

'Gee, maybe my age, something like that. You know, it's funny, he was wearing a motor driver's cap, like you see in the movies. He was holding a newspaper up close, and he had a handkerchief over his face, too, so it was hard to see.'

'And there was definitely only a single shot?'

'Only one. I did get the number of the car. Never forget it: 1556.'

The manner in which the policeman reacted to getting this piece of information helped settle Woodcock a little, and gradually he was able to recount the whole diabolical story. Davis was just about satisfied when Telford interrupted. 'I'm sorry constable, but we've got a filly in the second this afternoon. I've got to get her ready. Will that be all?'

'For the moment, sir. I expect a detective will be contacting you shortly. A constable will stay here to help guard Phar Lap. I think they'll be giving you an escort to the track.'

'They'd better be,' Telford responded. 'We're not going anywhere without you fellas.'

They both chuckled slightly at that, but only for the moment, and then Telford and Woodcock were out the door. David Davis remained; at least he was keen to talk.

BACK IN JANUARY 1928, Telford had convinced Davis, a brash American-born businessman, to bid sight unseen for a colt sired by the poorly performed English-bred stallion Night Raid out of a broken-down New Zealand mare named Entreaty, which was in the catalogue for the Trentham Thoroughbred Yearling Sales in New Zealand. Davis sent a representative to the sale and authorised him to bid no higher than 200 guineas, which proved more than enough, for the colt that would be named Phar Lap was knocked down for just 160 guineas. On the same day, a man representing the chairman of the Victoria Racing Club (VRC), Mr LKS Mackinnon, paid 2000 guineas for a colt to be named Carradale. Another colt, that would race as Honour, went for 2300 guineas.

Only trouble was, when his new purchase arrived in Sydney after a gruelling voyage across the Tasman, Davis took one look and rejected him outright. Telford, who was taken by the colt's breeding if not his appearance, came up with a compromise: he'd lease the horse for three years, covering all expenses and giving Davis one-third of any prizemoney. What prizemoney? It turned out to be the deal of a lifetime.

'I want to offer £100 to find the people responsible for this,' David Davis now told Senior Constable Davis. It probably didn't occur to him that such a sum wasn't much less than he'd paid for the horse in the first place.

'I think you'll have to do that down at the station. A detective should be here in a little while. I'm sure he'll be able to help you.'

'It's the ante-post betting that's responsible,' Davis continued, hardly drawing breath.

'The what?'

'The ante-post betting. The Cups double. The Caulfield and Melbourne Cups. If Phar Lap wins the Melbourne Cup, it'll break the bookies. I know that for a fact. You talk to the bookies, you'll find who tried to shoot my horse.'

The policeman promised to follow that up. He had to get down to the crime scene, so he excused himself, went out the back to tell Telford and Woodcock where he was going and tried not to worry that they didn't seem to care. Out the gate, he walked down Beverley Street to James Street and then up to Etna Street. There he was met by a solitary constable talking to bystanders and a small posse of journalists, the most assertive of whom was a fellow from the *Herald*, which wasn't surprising given that their first afternoon edition was due on the street at around 2pm. Senior Constable Davis was also aware of the paper's reputation, built over the previous decade, of making the most out of stories. It wasn't like the old days, when the papers used to just report what happened. Now they liked to 'sensationalise' things. A story like this, of gangsters brazenly trying to shoot the Cup favourite, would stay on the front page for days. Nothing surer.

Davis' job was to play along. Give the press what they want, no more, don't get yourself in trouble, was what he'd learned in 25 years as a policeman. So he offered them Woodcock's statement, pretty much word for word, told them about the likelihood of a reward, and then went looking for eyewitnesses.

THE FIRST PERSON TO talk to was Ronald Taylor, the paperboy. The 14-year-old had a big toothy grin, but the only time Davis saw it was when the *Herald* photographer asked the kid to smile as he took his picture for the afternoon's paper. Taylor explained how he saw Phar Lap and the man with him on the pony, how the man had brought Phar Lap round into Etna Street, and then the car came round, the gun went 'bang!' and then it sped off up the street, turned right and was gone. No, he hadn't seen the gunman. He wasn't sure what kind of car it was. He thought it was green, maybe blue.

The Bayley family, who lived at 8 James Street, right on the corner, had heard a shot but saw nothing. 'It was definitely a gun, not a car backfiring,' stated Mr Fred Bayley, who had been lying in bed when the incident occurred. A few excitable types claimed to have witnessed much, but after hearing their conflicting stories, clearly they hadn't seen a thing. Except Phar Lap in the flesh, which was thrilling enough. The reporters said that they'd found plenty of people who heard the gunfire and a few who'd eyeballed the car, and the general consensus was it was a Studebaker sedan, though a fellow from a nearby stable insisted it was a Buick.

A trainer, Joe Bird, who had stables in Manchester Grove, had been riding a horse and leading two others from the track back to his yard when he saw the car take off after Woodcock. The gun had been blasted two or three minutes before six o'clock. Bird had seen the car parked there when he set off for the track, about quarter past five, and thought it unusual. Then the *Herald* reporter pushed forward his paper's 'Caulfield track representative', one James Creed, who quietly told how, on his way to the course this morning he had seen the car parked outside the picture theatre and also thought it was strange, to the point that he noted the front number plate: 14750.

Other than that, though, Creed wasn't much use, and Davis was about to head back to Cripps' stables when he was approached by a bloke maybe 50 years old, dressed pretty much like Woodcock had been: sleeves rolled up, a battered old vest and a cloth cap, khaki trousers and heavy boots. He also had a cigarette in his hand. There were no pretensions about him; it was as if the term 'knockabout' had been invented for him.

'Excuse me, constable.'

'Senior constable.'

'Sorry, senior constable. I just thought I'd be able to help you.'

'How is that?'

'I work for Mr Piper, the trainer, up on Booran Road, backing onto Augusta Street. I was walking one of my boss's horses this morning, up near Glenhuntly Road, when a big car swung around from Glenhuntly Road into Augusta and nearly cleaned me up. It went flying down towards Beverley Street.'

'What kind of car? What time was that?'

'Definitely a Studebaker. I like them cars. About five past five. No, not about, definitely five past five. I left the stable at five o'clock.'

Senior Constable Davis noted Leonard Searle's name, thanked him for his assistance. He wished Searle had been more helpful, then he wondered, hadn't Woodcock said that he had been using Augusta Street to get Phar Lap to and from the track; that he only used James Street this morning, as a change of routine? Maybe the villains had been aiming to get the job done on the way to the track, not the journey home? Davis looked around and saw no more witnesses, only spectators. He figured it was time to go. But then he stopped, and called out, 'Mr Searle, do you mind? Just one more thing.'

'What's that?'

'Mr Searle, can you tell me ... why do you think they wanted to shoot Phar Lap?'

'It's the bookies, mate. The word's been out since Amounis won the Caulfield Cup. If Phar Lap wins the Melbourne Cup, it'll put 'em out of business. I mean, it wasn't them firing the gun. They'd have got someone else to do that. Go into any pub round here on a Thursday night and you'll have a driver and a shotgun in no time. The motor might be harder, but not much. You mightn't have that till the Friday morning.'

Davis thought of some of the seedier places he'd seen in his time, of poorly lit alleyways in the inner city he'd sneaked up to raid illegal gambling dens or sly grog shops. He remembered the dismal types who frequented those joints, men and even boys who'd be busted, bailed and back all in the same evening.

'I bet there are plenty of blokes around at the moment who can handle a shotgun and that'd take a pop at a horse for a few bob,' Searle continued. 'You'd have thought they would've got someone that could shoot straight, though, eh?'

'Maybe they weren't trying to kill Phar Lap, just scare him?'

'Make him bolt? Could've done. But I dunno, if they really wanted to put him out of business they'd have wanted to do more than just make him bolt.'

So it was the bookmakers. David Davis had been right. Now all two of Melbourne's finest detectives had to do was work out which ones.

CHAPTER THREE

PERCEPTIONS CAN BE EVERYTHING

JACK BROPHY WASN'T USED to feeling sorry for anyone, but he sure as hell felt sorry for Tommy Woodcock. The poor kid was terrified. It can't be good being constantly told by your boss that there's nothing to worry about — as Harry Telford kept repeating as they sat in the lounge room of Joe Cripps' house — when you've just had a shotgun pointed at you. It must also be hard to feel all right about yourself when everyone talks about the horse being shot at, and no one stops to think that you were between the horse and the business end of the gun at the time.

Still, Brophy only felt that pang of sympathy for a moment. He had work to do, and the first part of that assignment was to get Phar Lap to the races that afternoon. He thought about asking whether it might be better if the champion stayed in his stall, but his instincts told him that'd be pointless. Brophy enjoyed the races, knew a lot of racing people and liked them, felt he understood them. There was the Melbourne Stakes to win this afternoon, then the Melbourne Cup. If a trainer thought his horse needed the run on the Saturday to get him just right for the Cup on Tuesday, then no mug assassin was going to get in the way of that. Neither was Detective-Sergeant Jack Brophy.

Brophy had been a policeman for 30 years, a detective for the best part of 20. He'd only just met the minimum height requirement when he first signed up, and these days he carried more weight around his girth than was necessary, which made the flashy gold watch-chain attached to his vest all the more prominent. Usually, he was a jovial chap who loved a chat and could mix in all circles. For the first 25 years it had been the best job in the world, winning him respect among his colleagues, a certain notoriety in the city's underworld and not a little good publicity from the press. The high point had come in 1922, when with Detective-Sergeant Fred Piggott he'd solved the notorious 'Gun Alley Murder'. On New Year's Eve 1921, a 12-year-old girl, Alma Tirtschke, had been found outraged and strangled in a city lane. The murder was appalling, and all energies were devoted to solving the crime as quickly as possible, not least because the *Herald*'s new editor-in-chief, the celebrated war correspondent Keith Murdoch, was clamouring for an arrest. Within 13 days, Piggott and Brophy had their man, Colin Campbell Ross, and he was duly convicted and hanged. The process, all up, took 115 days and the result pleased just about everyone. The city was safe, the *Herald*'s sales rocketed (so much so that when the 'Herald and Weekly Times', the publishers of the *Herald*, moved soon after to new offices in Flinders Street, the premises became known as 'the house that Ross built') and the two detectives became celebrities of a sort.

The only loser in the affair was Colin Ross, who might well have been innocent. Some people strongly suggested that evidence used in the trial had been twisted or fabricated. But whenever this was put to Jack Brophy, he was indignant. 'Mate, our job is to put the bastards behind bars,' he'd snap. 'It's not how we do it, but that we do it.'

In 1925, things started to go slightly awry. A new police commissioner, the decorated war hero Brigadier-General Thomas Blamey, was appointed on the recommendation of the Inspector-General of the Australian Military Forces, Sir Harry Chauvel. Neither the government nor the Melbourne Establishment could forget the anarchy that came with the infamous police strike of 1923, which they blamed at least in part on the weak leadership of the previous commissioner, Alexander Nicholson. They wanted a strong man who'd put the radicals in their place, and the decisive and well-organised General Blamey was perfect. Jack Brophy was hardly a bleeding heart, and he quickly realised his philosophy on life and the service matched that of the new man in charge. However, this put him offside with many of his colleagues, who saw Blamey as being against the working class from which most of them came. Brophy quit the Victorian Police Association in protest at what he said were his colleagues' narky, self-serving attitudes, an act which might have won him a few friends in very high places, but also cost him some friendships down the line. Occasionally, being a copper wasn't fun any more.

By November 1930, only one thing was certain: this Cup favourite was not going to die on his watch, even if the first thing he thought when he was told the gunman had missed was that he was dealing with amateurs. He'd read about the storm Telford had created when he scratched Phar Lap from the Caulfield Cup, and he wanted to know if the rumours that Telford or people close to him were going to make a lot of money out of the Cups double were fair dinkum. Enough to kill a horse? If the gossip was true, who had they been punting with? And who was this American who kept butting in about a bloody reward?

'David Davis is my name. I'm the owner of Phar Lap. Mr Telford leases him from me. The constable who was here earlier suggested you would be the man to talk to.'

'Indeed I am, sir,' Brophy replied. He was in many ways the epitome of the modern policeman, able to mix with all types, speak their languages. Some of his colleagues at the CIB (Criminal Investigation Branch) didn't appreciate that. He could have put Davis in his place, but that wouldn't have been right.

'I think that is certainly a worthwhile idea, Mr Davis. What sort of reward were you considering?'

'Ah, £100.'

'Very good. I will organise for the appropriate document to be drawn up. Can you call into our Russell Street headquarters on your way to the races this afternoon and sign it then?'

'Um, very well. Do you need anything else from me?'

'No. Thank you, Mr Davis.'

The silence made it clear he was no longer welcome. With a curt nod to Brophy and even less acknowledgement to Harry Telford, Davis departed.

Now Brophy could talk to Phar Lap's trainer, the man whose job it was to prepare the great horse for his racetrack engagements. First, the senior detective introduced his partner, Detective Harold Saker, who had spent a few minutes at the crime scene before rushing down to Beverley Street, and then he started asking questions.

'Why would someone want to shoot your horse, Mr Telford?'

'I dunno. Lots of people are jealous.'

'Of what, sir? Most of us love a great horse.'

'Maybe not one this good.'

Brophy had been told Telford could be a difficult man, but quickly he sensed that the fidgety old horseman was actually more shy than cold. He saw across the table a bloke who wasn't quite sure what was going on, who feared that whatever he did next would be a mistake. That, of course, included talking to the police. What Harry Telford desperately needed, thought Jack Brophy, was a friend.

'Mr Telford, do you want us to find the people who tried to shoot your horse?'

'Get me through to Tuesday, Detective-Sergeant, and I'll be happy.'

'Winning the Cup means that much to you?'

Telford looked up when Brophy asked that question. Someone had finally cut to the core of it all. All his racecourse acquaintances had assumed it was about the money.

'They won't be able to knock me any more if he wins the Cup.'

Brophy understood that. He'd always marvelled at the way the Cup got *everyone* in, how some people almost seemed to measure time by Cup winners. He'd started in the force in 1900, Clean Sweep's year. He joined the CIB in 1912, Piastre's year, became a senior detective in 1921, Sister Olive's year. Interstate jealousies were forgotten on Cup Day, when the bloke from the outback could stand as one with the suit from the city. For a day, maybe just for the race itself, your worries were over. The Cup had become Australia's obsession. He'd heard how workers in the far north would ride 50 miles because they wanted to experience the race on a wireless, knowing full well that the reception might be terrible or non-existent. How people used to wait in the thousands outside newspaper offices in Sydney, Adelaide, Perth, everywhere, waiting for the result to be posted on a big notice board. How the company director and the girl on reception had an equal chance of winning the office 'Cup sweep', in which you bought a ticket and got a runner drawn out of a hat. How fathers who day after day preached about the evils of gambling suddenly asked their children on the morning of the big race, 'What do you like in the Cup?'

The Melbourne Cup had been the idea of Captain Frederick Charles Standish, a committeeman of the long defunct Victoria Turf Club, in 1861. The VTC and the Victoria Jockey Club, at the time co-tenants of Melbourne's principal racetrack — at Flemington in the city's north — had been involved in something of a race of their own. In 1850, the VTC introduced a St Leger Stakes, mimicking the celebrated English race, and five years later they ran the first Victoria Derby which quickly became one of the classic races of the Australian turf — a race for three-year-olds, run at 'set weights' over a mile and a half. In 1857, the VJC ran a St Leger and a Victoria Derby of their own, and in 1861 they launched the inaugural Victoria Oaks Stakes. The obvious thing for the VTC to do was counter with their own Oaks, but instead Standish proposed a two-mile handicap, to be the richest race of the year and known as the Melbourne Cup. Not everyone liked the idea, with one racing writer arguing, 'To make a handicap the principal event of the turf year is to make a farce of everything that racing stands for.'

However, the notion of equality that handicapping provides became a key factor in the race's unique appeal. It became the quintessential Australian event, appealing at the same time to the nation's love of sport and its 'fair go' and 'have a go' philosophies.

The Cup nearly fizzled after only seven runners greeted the judge in 1863, but the following year the two squabbling clubs merged to become the Victoria Racing Club, and the new body had the good sense to continue with the Cup as the premier race of the year. By 1880, Grand Flaneur's year, Cup Day was luring 100,000 patrons to Flemington. At the time, the population of Melbourne was around 280,000.

The Cup became a race that made or tarnished reputations. Great horses such as The Barb (1866), Poseidon (1906) and Poitrel (1920) established themselves as true champions with their Cup victories, while others with arguably greater claims to legendary status were not quite so royally regarded purely because they failed to win the nation's biggest race. Trafalgar, Eurythmic and Manfred were excellent examples of this. Aurum, a colt that carried 8 stone 6 pounds (8.6), an unbelievable weight for a three-year-old, would be straight into racing's hall of fame rather than forgotten if he'd finished first instead of third in 1897. Phar Lap carried a full stone less when he ran third in 1929. Jim Pike, Phar Lap's regular rider, had never won the Cup, which for some meant he wasn't a great jockey. Critics could ignore all the fantastic races Pike had won over the years and sneer about the mistake he made in 1926, Spearfelt's year, when he took off on Pantheon too far from home and was run down in the last half furlong.

Cup stories of triumph, heartbreak, mystery and humour abounded. People had made and lost tens of thousands on the race, dreamt of the winner months before, paid a fortune for the second horse, sold the winner for a song. In 1882, a former premier of Tasmania, the Hon. Thomas Reibey, owner of four-year-old Stockwell and three-year-old Bagot, asked a psychic about his two horses' chances in the big race, and was told that Bagot would win the Cup. This was no good, because he and his friends had backed Stockwell, so he scratched the younger horse, watched Stockwell run second to The Assyrian and then sold Bagot to Mr JO Inglis, who promptly renamed the colt Malua. In

1884, Malua won the Cup, which sort of proved the fortune teller right. When a woman gave birth in the doctor's room of the Members Stand during the running of the 1894 Cup, won by Patron, she and her husband named their new daughter 'Patrona'. It was lucky this didn't happen in Windbag's year.

For Harry Telford, the Melbourne Cup was his chance to finally shake the 'battling trainer' tag for good. Ever since Phar Lap first showed some ability he was fixated with the idea that winning the Cup was the way to do that. If anyone wanted to have a go at him after that, he could wear the scorn and then go home, look at the three-handled trophy on the mantelpiece, and reassure himself that he was okay. It was about respect — from others and, more importantly, in his own mind.

'So why would you risk all that by cooking the Cups double?' Brophy asked.

'I've heard a lot of things about the doubles betting, Detective-Sergeant, but I'll be buggered if know what's the truth and what isn't,' Telford began. 'Once the horse started winning I had all sorts hanging round my stable, and people suggesting all kinds of fancy schemes for getting rich. But I was already making more money than I ever dreamed of, just by Phar Lap winning all the time. I'm getting two-thirds of the prizemoney! You know, I was stone broke before he won his first race. If he hadn't won that day, I was gone.'

'You don't mind a bet, Mr Telford?' Brophy asked.

'I don't like betting with money I ain't got. I've seen too many people get hurt doing that. But I don't owe the bookies anything.'

Telford paused. For a moment he was going to tell the detective about his filly in the second race at Flemington. However, his natural caution got the better of him.

'Have you backed Phar Lap in the Melbourne Cup?' Detective Saker asked.

'Nah, he's too short, way too short. He was 6–1 before the weights come out,' Telford said. Every year, the handicaps for the two big Cups were released on June 30, more than four months before the jump. A lot can go wrong in that time, so it was unprecedented for the bookies to be so cautious.

'So why did you leave it so late to scratch him from the Caulfield Cup?' Brophy inquired. He read the racing pages in the papers every day, and knew what a storm Telford's actions had caused.

Telford had never revealed this to anyone, but right at this moment talking was doing him good. 'Like Mr Davis said before, I'm only leasing the horse, and my lease runs out at the start of February. Davis wasn't even going to let me train him after that. So I figured, if I've only got him until then, I'd better make the most of it. I would've run at Caulfield, in the Melbourne Cup, then gone to Perth, run him in a couple of races over there. Davis wanted me to save him for next year, but what's the point of that, I thought? I've made this horse, I told him, you should respect me for that. I told him I wasn't scratching him from anything until we had a deal, and he didn't come round to my way of thinking till the Sunday before the Caulfield Cup. Monday morning, I got it in writing, and I went straight down to the scratchings office, got there just in time.

'The word is that someone plonked plenty on the Amounis–Phar Lap double knowing you were going to scratch your horse,' Brophy said, repeating what had become one of the strongest rumours in town. 'By leaving Phar Lap in until the last minute, they got top odds.'

'I dunno whether Davis left it that late to make money on the double, or whether he used me to get a price, and I don't care,' Telford shot back. 'I never asked him. The press can say what they like.'

SO WHAT WAS THIS 'Cups double' that was causing such consternation? The Caulfield Cup and the Melbourne Cup were the two principal handicap races run in Australia every spring, the Caulfield race being run 17 days before the first Tuesday in November. The handicapper's principal objective was, by way of weights, to try to give every horse in a race an equal chance of winning. A handicapper's dream was for every horse to flash across the finish line together.

The horse rated the best by the handicapper was given the most weight. An old racing cliché was that 'weight could stop a train', which reflected the undeniable fact that only the champion horses could overcome huge handicaps. Indeed, there had only been five instances of the 'top weight' (the horse with the heaviest load to carry) winning the Melbourne Cup: Archer (in 1862), Warrior (1869), Carbine (1890), Poitrel (1920) and Spearfelt (equal top weight in 1926). The unheralded Banker won in 1863 with just 5.4, a full six stone less than the weight given to Archer, the horse bred at Braidwood in country New South Wales that had famously won the first two Cups. (Unfortunately, Archer didn't get the chance to win a third Cup. The 'intention to run' form his owner-trainer, Edwin de Mestre, sent in 1863 arrived in Melbourne on a public holiday, and when the messenger loitered the following day, the paperwork didn't get to the Victoria Turf Club's offices until after the deadline for the forms to arrive had closed.) Archer (10.2), Carbine (10.5) and Poitrel (10.0) were the only three horses to carry 10 stone or more to victory. Phar Lap, a four-year-old, had been allocated 9.12 for the 1930 Melbourne Cup. The most weight carried by a four-year-old to victory in the Cup's first 69 editions was 9.3, by Patron in 1894.

When the weights for the Caulfield and Melbourne Cups were announced each year there were inevitably many entrants in the two races that appeared to have a real chance of winning. This usually remained true during July, August and September, as some good horses lost form but a number of previously mediocre or unknown gallopers suddenly improved to take their place at or near the top of the betting markets. Some owners of high-class gallopers took their time to decide if they'd run in the big Cups or set their sights elsewhere. Perhaps they didn't like the weight the handicapper had given them for the Cup. All this meant that if you 'took' a double — trying to find the winners of the two races — a bookmaker would usually offer very good odds about you being right, especially if you made the bet weeks out from the Caulfield Cup.

The odds (or 'price') on offer at any time essentially reflect a bookmaker's assessment of each horse's chances in a race. A horse considered to have little chance of winning will be a 'long' price; a favourite will be at a 'short' price. Thus, a bookmaker is said to 'shorten' (or 'tighten') a horse's odds if he believes the galloper's chances have improved, and 'lengthen' (or 'ease') those odds if his information says the horse's chances have declined. If a bookie thinks a horse has a one-in-two, or 50 per cent, chance of winning a race he will offer odds of 1–1 (even money, or 'evens'). A one-in-three chance (33.33 percent) is 2–1, one-in-five (20 per cent) is 4–1, and so on. A horse at odds of 100–1 has very little chance of winning (though The Pearl won the Cup at precisely that price in 1871); an 'odds on' runner has more chance than the rest of the field put together. Reality says that the total odds on offer should add up to 100 per cent, but the bookies try to 'frame' their prices to add up to between 105 and 120 per cent, so in the long run they should make a profit. Punters make their own judgements, often rating a horse's chances differently to a bookmaker. The betting ring is essentially a free market where these different opinions come together, with the bookmakers offering prices about each horse's chances and the punters accepting or rejecting those prices. If the bookmakers are better judges than the punters, they'll make money; over the years, both punters and bookies had been known to use deceptive and dishonourable tactics to gain an advantage.

With the Cups double, if, for example, a punter selected a 5–1 chance in the Caulfield Cup and a 10–1 chance in the Melbourne Cup, a doubles bookmaker might offer him odds of 65–1 about his two selections winning — on the basis that a pound on a 5–1 winner would give the punter £6 (including the original stake of £1) and if that £6 went on a 10–1 winner he'd be collecting £66. If you wanted to back the same horse in both legs, the price on offer was always shorter, on the basis that the winner of the Caulfield Cup always started at fairly tight odds if he ran in the Melbourne Cup. Not every bookie was as brave or generous as the next, so it was part of the game to shop around to make sure you secured the best odds available. Over the years, it had become almost an art form for a trainer to disguise the true ability of a good horse, so it would get into one or both of the Cups with a relatively light weight, and be at a long price until the bets were on. A flood of money for a particular horse or a marked form improvement — one often being related to the other — would force a bookmaker to reconsider his original assessment of a Cup entry's chances. In the bookmakers' favour was the fact that betting was 'all in'. If a horse was scratched, for whatever reason, any money wagered stayed in the bookies' bags.

The Amounis–Phar Lap double was a different proposition from most, in that when the weights came out for the 1930 Cups, the two horses' great ability was well known and had been for quite some time. Both were required to break weight-carrying records to win the Cups they'd been set for. Amounis was trained by one of the best in the business — Frank McGrath, who'd won the Melbourne Cup with Prince Foote in 1909 — and had won races as a three-year-old through until he was eight, 16 of them at weight-for-age plus a Rosehill Guineas, two Epsom Handicaps, two Cantala Stakes and the Gold Cup at Wagga Wagga. From not long after the weights had been issued for the two Cups, he was one of the favourites for the Caulfield Cup. Bookmakers refused to take too many risks with Phar Lap for that race either, even though most doubted that Telford would risk gaining a weight penalty for the Melbourne Cup by running him at Caulfield. However, successive defeats for Amounis in the Memsie Stakes and a mediocre Moonee Valley handicap, a string of emphatic wins for Phar Lap in Sydney, and the simple fact that Telford refused to rule out a start for his champion in the Caulfield Cup meant that by late September many punters had changed their minds about Phar Lap. He became the new Caulfield Cup favourite.

Amounis promptly won two more weight-for-age races, the October Stakes and the Caulfield Stakes, and after Telford finally went to the scratchings office at Caulfield, the gossip was that the people with an ear in both camps had placed big bets on the right double at the right time. The suspicion that Telford had been up to no good was heightened when at first he blamed the late scratching on the NSW and Victorian Railways, saying they'd mucked up Phar Lap's transfer from one train to another at Albury on the gelding's trip south. When the railway commissioner angrily refuted that, Telford changed his story, now explaining to reporters that his foreman, who was travelling with the horse, had made the decision to break up the trip. That was news to Tommy Woodcock, who'd actually done as he was told. There was no doubt the Phar Lap camp had brought the wrath of the public, the bookies and the press upon themselves.

Perceptions can be everything. The *Sporting Globe's* story of Phar Lap's scratching was headlined 'Public Are Fooled Again' while the *Sydney Sportsman* led with 'Poor Punters Paralysed'. The Melbourne *Truth* went this way: 'Books Reap Harvest Over Phar Lap'. This reflected a fact quickly forgotten amid all the hysteria over the Cups doubles: the bookmakers were hardly destroyed in the immediate aftermath of the 1930 Caulfield Cup. A win by the favourite is rarely a good result for the bookies, and they were undoubtedly facing big payouts on the Amounis–Phar Lap double, but after Telford scratched his horse they collected all the money that had been bet on Phar Lap to win the Caulfield Cup, a considerable amount on the 'Phar Lap–Phar Lap' double and more still on any other double that began with Phar Lap. Then, on the Monday after the Caulfield Cup, the New Zealand galloper Glare, which had been a well-supported second favourite for the Melbourne Cup, was withdrawn from all spring engagements after suffering an injury. The bookies won again.

'YEAH, I'VE HEARD ALL about that Amounis double,' Telford muttered to Brophy and Saker. 'As well as that, do you know Nightmarch only went back home after the Sydney carnival because I told his trainer we were definitely going to run in the Caulfield Cup? That I scared them off? That's what they're saying! But Nightmarch's owner wants to win the New Zealand Cup, I know that for a fact, and that's run the Saturday after the Melbourne Cup. That's why he went home. If he wanted to run in the New Zealand Cup, he had to go straight back after the Sydney carnival, not go via Caulfield and Flemington.'

The allegation that Telford scared Nightmarch out of the Caulfield Cup to get a better price about Amounis in the Caulfield Cup had quickly become one of the great myths of Australian racing, despite the fact that a simple analysis showed that it couldn't be true. Nightmarch, the New Zealand Derby winner of 1928, had been the star of the spring of 1929, winning the Epsom Handicap in Sydney before coming south to claim the Cox Plate and then the Melbourne Cup by four lengths, leaving even Phar Lap, the even-money favourite, in his wake. But after that, whenever Phar Lap and Nightmarch met, Telford's horse won easily. At the recent Sydney carnival they'd clashed five times, and each time Phar Lap had finished in front of Nightmarch, usually many lengths in front.

At their most recent meeting, in the mile-and-a-quarter Craven Plate at Randwick on October 4, Roy Reed on Nightmarch had decided to take Phar Lap on. He did this after punters linked to the New Zealand stable, including a high-profile Sydney punter named Eric Connolly, plonked plenty on their galloper, apparently convinced that Telford's horse was a query if tested from the start. Unfortunately, they were misinformed — Phar Lap won in Australasian record time — but given their activity in the betting ring, it is hard to believe that before the Craven Plate Nightmarch's connections were totally convinced that Phar Lap was unbeatable, that there was no point taking him on in the Caulfield Cup or Melbourne Cup. All the big bets on the double reputedly went on in late September. The fact was that almost all the New Zealand-based horses that raced in Sydney during the spring of 1930, including Nightmarch and the 1929 Melbourne Cup runner-up, Paquito, returned home immediately afterwards so they could compete at the New Zealand Cup carnival.

'You've got to believe some of the rumours about bookmakers going broke, I suppose,' Telford continued. 'But I don't think they're in as much trouble as what some people reckon. The bloke who's supposed to be behind the doubles coup, he always talks himself up. And when they were supposed to put the bets on, the odds weren't that great. They say 40–1, but, you know, I wonder. I can find you a doubles card I've got somewhere from September 23 that has the Amounis–Phar Lap double as a "special" at 20–1. Amounis wasn't going so well in September; looked like he might have been over the hill.'

'And Amounis is hopeless in the wet,' Brophy added.

'That's right. If it'd rained on Caulfield Cup day they'd have done the lot.'

'So you don't think the bookies would try and stop your horse?'

'They might. It could be a punter, maybe somebody just doesn't like me,' Telford hadn't talked this much in his life. 'You read the papers and it's not safe to walk the streets any more. In Sydney, it's razors, down here it's shotguns. We got threats last year, you know. We guarded him day and night then and we've been doing the same now. It's not easy out there, with all them people out of work. Racetrack's no different to the rest of the world. I've been getting letters and phone calls, but I wasn't sure it was all that serious. I was worried someone might try and dope him, get some drugs in his feed or something, throw acid in his face, so I got myself an extra guard dog and have been using this face mask to protect him. Thought that'd do it. But after this morning ... Jeez, they really are out to get me.'

At the Moonee Valley Cup meeting a week after the Caulfield Cup, Phar Lap's victory in the Cox Plate had been greeted in silence, and Telford had been hooted by some spectators when he showed his face in the mounting yard. Seven days on, he wondered what sort of welcome he'd receive today at Flemington. Would the sympathy be with the shooters or the shot at?

'When do you have to go to the course?' Brophy knew time was getting short.

'I've got one in race two, at 2.20. She's got a chance, might be a good price, too. I'd like her to be there with plenty of time to spare, and the traffic'll be rough, so we'll be out of here about half eleven. Phar Lap's running at three. What do you reckon? I guess we should leave him here as late as possible, leave about one o'clock?'

'That's pretty tight, but it should be right,' Brophy replied. He tugged at his watch-chain, and saw it was already a quarter to 11. He had wanted to duck down to the crime scene, to check it out for himself, but not to worry, he could do that after the races, after they'd got Phar Lap safely home. Telford called in Stan Boyden, the float driver, and introduced him to the detectives, who then outlined exactly what security arrangements would be in place. Boyden was a man to be trusted and quite a horseman — he'd been stable foreman for trainer Vin O'Neill when Spearfelt won the VRC Derby and ran an unlucky third to Backwood and Stand By in the 1924 Cup, and when he won the Cup two years later.

Two detectives would go to the races with the float, which would be escorted by four other policemen on motor bikes. Brophy and Saker would meet the float when it arrived at the track. Phar Lap's stall would be guarded and he'd be escorted all the way from the birdcage, the enclosure where horses on race day were stabled, to the mounting yard, where the horses paraded before going onto the track, to the course proper and down to the start. Let's get him to the course as late as possible and get him out of there as quick as we can. We'll have men down the back straight, so no one can have a shot at him down there. We'll also leave a constable here, so no one can do anything while we're gone. It all sounded pretty good; Telford was as confident as he could be that they'd look after his horse. He thanked Brophy and Saker for the chat and excused himself to go and get ready for the track, while Boyden and Woodcock returned to the horses.

The two detectives found themselves alone in the lounge room, but only for a moment, because soon Senior Constable Davis walked in to join them. From the corner of James and Etna, Davis had returned to Glenhuntly Police Station to tell his immediate superiors what he'd discovered. Now he was back to go through his notes for the detectives' benefit and find out what he should do next. That, he soon learnt, was to stay put, to keep an eye on the horse. But before he ducked outside, Saker asked him one more question:

'Senior Constable, did you see any evidence up at Etna Street that a shot was fired?'

'Ah, no sir,' Davis replied.

'I'm going to have to go back up there, have a good look around,' Saker muttered. 'What are you going to do, Jack?'

'I want to make a couple of calls,' Brophy replied. 'See if anyone's heard anything. And I have to ring my bookie. I've got a tip for a filly in the second on Derby Day.'

CHAPTER FOUR

THEY INTENDED TO KILL HIM

IF THE HOODLUMS IN the Studebaker parked outside the Glenhuntly picture theatre had been reading their newspapers, they would have learned that the Commonwealth meteorologist, Mr Hunt, expected 'summery skies' to continue throughout Derby Day. Elsewhere in the *Sun News-Pictorial*, 'experts' were quoted as saying that Flemington had 'never looked better' than for the 1930 spring carnival. The paper's correspondent continued:

> Special rose displays around the lawns should attract thousands of garden lovers whose lesser interest will lie with the racing.
>
> Many hot-house blooms, nurtured under the direction of the curator (Mr E.H. Hill) in the Flemington conservatory, will form the basis of the interior decorations. Stronger plants will adorn the stands.

Heavy Cup week bookings, well up to the average of prosperous years, are reported from leading city hotels. Many guests have already arrived, but today will probably bring the largest influx of visitors with the arrival of the *Manunda* from Fremantle and Adelaide, and interstate and country trains.

Sydney has sent the biggest contingent by car, steamer, train and even aeroplane. The Melbourne manager of Australian National Airways (Mr Young) said yesterday that many people were taking advantage of the innovation of flying to the Melbourne Cup for the first time ...

On the Friday evening, the *Herald* had reported that 'unusual activity is reported by those shops which specially cater for women'. The economic downturn that had impaired the Australian economy for the past three years and turned dismal with the Stock Exchange crash of 1929 might have put a dampener on some regular Cup festivities, but the city and its people were still coming to life. 'Leading frock shops are working at top pressure,' the *Herald*'s writer added. 'Some have even had to engage extra hands, who are working day and night to supply the demand for race gowns. These will be gayer than usual. If the weather is fine, floral fabrics of brilliant hues will be seen. Yellow will be the prevailing and fashionable colour. Long frocks and shady, floppy hats will be the fine weather "note".'

At 10.30 on the Saturday, while Jack Brophy and Harry Telford were talking in Joe Cripps' lounge room, the first race train departed Spencer Street station in the city. Special tickets admitting patrons onto trains and into Flemington were available at all stations within a 27-mile radius of Melbourne, and also from the regional centres of Geelong, Ballarat and Bendigo. The race-day trams didn't start until 11.30am, just as

Telford and his filly La Justice were setting off for the course, but for a period from not long after midday they were scheduled to run at 90-second intervals. As the punters travelled to the track they could ponder a race day in which 14 Melbourne Cup contenders would be spread over four races: Balloon King, Veilmond and Wapilly in the Victoria Derby; Carradale, Donald, Phar Lap and Tregilla in the Melbourne Stakes; Soulton in the Cantala Stakes; and First Acre, John Buchan, Muratti, Second Wind, Some Quality and Temptation in the Hotham Handicap. The only Cup entrants not appearing would be the Moonee Valley Cup winner Shadow King, the handy South Australian stayer Nadean and Star God, whose owner, a Mr Hadley, conceded had next to no chance of winning. He was going to scratch him until contacted by a man who explained he had drawn Star God in a major Cup sweepstake. Money changed hands and the horse stayed in the race.

Those who sneered at this development were quickly reminded of Posinatus, the Sydney horse that won the Cup in 1913, but only after a punter put up the money to get the horse to Melbourne. This man had dreamt that Aurifer, as No. 5, would win the Caulfield Cup and Posinatus, as No. 8, would win the Melbourne Cup and backed the double to win £30,000. Even when Aurifer won at Caulfield wearing the five saddlecloth, the bookies weren't too concerned, because Posinatus had no form and a relatively light weight in the Cup. But then there were scratchings, sure enough Posinatus became No. 8, and he won by three-quarters of a length.

The early commuters to the track who were unaware of the Phar Lap shooting might have focused their conversations on the day's racing and how it might influence the big race on Tuesday. Derby Day was usually a good one for punters, never more so than in 1924 when the favourite won all six races. Those familiar with Cup history knew that while the Cantala Stakes was unlikely to throw any light on the bigger picture, the other three races might prove plenty. The Victoria Derby winner had gone on to win the Cup 11 times, been placed in the Cup five times in the previous six years, 14 times in the previous 31 years. Just two horses, Malua in 1884 and Carbine in 1890, had completed the Melbourne Stakes–Melbourne Cup double, but 14 horses had finished second or third in the Melbourne Stakes on the Saturday before winning the Cup on the Tuesday. The one Hotham Handicap winner to win the Cup in the previous 20 years had been King Ingoda in 1922, but two other Cup winners from the previous 12 years — Night Watch in 1918 and Backwood in 1924 — had been placed in the Hotham.

As the trains filled and the clock moved closer to midday, the stunned whispers about what had happened to Phar Lap grew louder. Details were scant, just repeats of the snippets that had been heard on the wireless that morning, or the gossip that a mate of a mate might have known. It was not until people started swapping stories on their arrival at the course, that reports of the scandal began to spread like a locust swarm.

Throughout the afternoon, the *Herald* had the story as a front-page lead. Later editions fleshed out the story, and featured a photo re-creation of the Studebaker's passage down Etna Street, and photos of 'Tom' Woodcock — now known to *Herald* readers as 'the man who saved Phar Lap' — and the paperboy. By the time Jack Brophy got his hands on a copy, just after two o'clock, Phar Lap had arrived at the track. The detective was astonished to discover that at least in some respects, the paper knew more about the incident than he did ...

ATTEMPT TO SHOOT PHAR LAP

Gun Fired From Moving Car In Street

RIDER'S CARE SAVES HORSE;
POLICE TO GUARD FAVOURITE UNTIL CUP

A DESPERATE attempt to shoot the Melbourne Cup favorite was made early today as the champion was being taken to the trainer's stables from his track work at Caulfield racecourse.

Two men in a car drove up to the horse near the corner of James and Etna Streets, Caulfield, and one fired a shotgun point blank.

The presence of mind of his attendant 'Tom' Woodcock saved the horse. Seeing the gun, he jammed Phar Lap against a house fence and screened him with the grey pony he was riding. The shot went wide and Phar Lap was not affected in any way.

The owner of Phar Lap, Mr D. J. Davis, has offered £100 reward for the conviction of the culprits.

Following this, Phar Lap is to be given a special police guard until he runs in the Cup on Tuesday.

EYE WITNESSES DESCRIBE INCIDENT

Phar Lap, who is leased from his owner, Mr D.J. Davis, by H.R. Telford, the trainer, is a hot favorite for the Melbourne Cup, to be run on Tuesday. He has been coupled in doubles for huge amounts with the Caulfield Cup winner Amounis. Last year, when he ran third, Phar Lap started a very warm favorite for the Cup.

Detective Saker is in charge of the police investigations. At least one of the assailants — of whom there were two — was seen, and is described as a fair, fat man. The car was a large Studebaker sedan of the latest model, the color being dark-bluish green or greenish-blue.

From now on, Phar Lap will be under continual police protection. A constable will be in his stalls at the trainer's stables the whole time. A particularly fierce kelpie dog is kept at the stable yards. Hitherto, the dog has worn a wire muzzle, but tonight the muzzle will be removed ...

On his way to the Caulfield racecourse early today The Herald track representative (Mr James Creed) saw at 5.5am [sic] what he described as a new bluish-colored sedan car. It attracted his attention, he said, for a number of reasons, one of them being the crude nature of the back lettering on the number plate, which showed 14750. He made a note of the back number, but did not note the front number.

Woodcock made a mental note of the number on the front number plate of the car from which the shot was fired. It showed 1556, also in crude lettering apparently done in paint, whitewash or chalk.

Norman Taylor, 14, newsboy, also saw the car from which the shot was fired, but did not make a note of the number.

Mr Creed's description of the car and Woodcock's tally in other respects, as also do their stories of the appearance and demeanor of the men in the car. Mr Creed said that although there were always many cars in the vicinity of the Caulfield racecourse gates, they were cars that belonged to trainers and jockeys that were there regularly. This one attracted his attention particularly because it was a new car, had not been in the vicinity before so far as he knew, was not parked with the other cars and had taken up a position from which the occupants had a clear view of the route which Phar Lap would usually take from the stables to the course. Moreover, it had taken up a position 300 yards from the course, which was unusual at that time of the morning.

Mr Creed said that he thought it was part of the precaution taken by Telford to protect the champion. But it seemed very strange to him that the man in the driver's seat was alone and put a newspaper up in front of his face when Creed passed. Another man seated in the back also hid his face behind a newspaper.

Mr Creed did not report his suspicions to Telford. For one thing, he did not meet him on the track, and for another he did not wish to perturb him with what appeared at the time to be only an imaginary danger ...

The *Herald*'s remarkably detailed report continued with Woodcock's description of the shooting, exactly as per Senior Constable Davis' inquiries. The second half of the story featured 'quotes' from 'Norman' Taylor and Mr Bayley and his daughter Freda, to whom Taylor was about to deliver a paper when the Studebaker rushed by. The front-page story ended with grabs from a brief interview with Harry Telford conducted outside Cripps' stables before he left for Flemington ...

'The horse is well and will start in the Stakes today. I'm taking every care of him, and he will be under close supervision from now until the Melbourne Cup starts. I am satisfied that they intended to kill him — the best horse in Australia.

'HOW LONG HAVE YOU been in charge of the investigation?' Brophy was looking straight at Saker. His partner simply shrugged his shoulders, and they both had a chuckle. Saker, not quite 40 years old, slightly taller and fitter than his senior partner, was another of the city's top detectives. When the Prince of Wales had visited Melbourne in 1920, Saker was given the task of looking after him. 'His Royal Highness' personal bodyguard' was how he rather proudly described that job. Another time, at the races, he saw the notorious mobster, Leslie 'Squizzy' Taylor, making a nuisance of himself in the betting ring. Saker knew that the diminutive Squizzy had been warned off Melbourne racetracks, so he decided to do the race club's job for it by escorting him off the course.

'You can't do that,' Squizzy protested.

'Yes, I can,' Saker replied, 'I'm charging you with vagrancy.'

'But I'm no vagrant. Look at all the money in me pockets.'

Squizzy's information that day had been impeccable and he was well in front on the punt. So the charge was possessing stolen goods, or theft, it didn't matter. Soon Squizzy, Saker and a few of Squizzy's disreputable underlings were outside the course, and Squizzy said, 'Where's your car?'

'I haven't got a car,' muttered Saker. 'We're short at the moment. We're catching the tram.'

'You're kidding! Let's get a taxi,' was Squizzy's retort.

'Can't afford it on my salary,' said the detective.

'Don't worry,' laughed the gangster, a man once described by the *Sun News-Pictorial* as the 'Beau Brummell of the Underworld'. 'I'll cover it.'

When they got to Russell Street, Squizzy told the cabbie to hang on. Saker led him inside, charged him, but Squizzy soon made bail. A little later, when Saker returned to the track, the first person he saw, inevitably, was Squizzy, who'd got the taxi back, which was much quicker than the detective's tram.

Six days before Trivalve's Cup in 1927, Taylor had been shot dead in a bloody gunfight with another notorious figure, John 'Snowy' Cutmore. Cutmore died, too, and the double murder shook Melbourne, because it so vividly demonstrated just how pitiless and brutal the local underworld could be. Three years later, Saker had been recognised by reporters soon after he left Cripps' stables to return to Etna Street, but that didn't stop him being surprised that his name appeared so prominently in the *Herald's* front-page story.

'Senior Constable Davis says you've got the cartridge case from the gun,' Brophy said to him, now deadly serious.

'Jack, if I had the cartridge case, that'd mean I was in the bloody car when the gun went off!' Saker responded. 'I've got a cardboard wad. A trainer called Joe Bird found it. He'd been at least a couple of hundred yards behind Woodcock when the shot was fired. I had a good yarn to him, but everything he saw was from a distance. After that, I didn't have much of a chance to look around — the press boys were still there, and a lot of people, too. You know, if we were fair dinkum, we really needed someone to close off the area. Straightaway when I got there, I had a bloke from the *Truth* ask me if we'd found any evidence of a shot being fired, and I said, "Not yet." He wrote that down real quick.'

'You did find some pellet marks eventually? Brophy asked.

'Well, no, that was the crazy thing,' Saker replied. 'I was half expecting to find a big bloody hole in the fence and the reporters were all asking me to show them where the bullets were, but I couldn't find anything.'

'Maybe the bloke in the car just fired up into the air.'

'The best I could do was to tell them that I'd show them all the evidence when I was good and ready.'

'What do you make of the *Herald's* story?' Brophy had to change the subject. Things often move quickly at the track on a race day, especially one as big as this. There was an awful lot to do.

What jumped out of the newspaper front page for Saker were the quotes from the paper's track representative. The way Senior Constable Davis had told it, James Creed could offer little. But judging by what was in the paper it now seemed that Creed might have got a better look at the men in the Studebaker than Woodcock.

'I know Telford was helpful, but the only person who's *really* keen to talk to us is the American owner,' Saker sighed. 'I saw him at the station before I came here. As soon as the reward letter was signed, he was out the door looking for a reporter. It wouldn't surprise me if he's had more conversations with pressmen in the last six hours than he's had with Telford in the past six months.'

Indeed, Davis would be quoted in the racing pages of the *Herald's* late editions. 'We received information yesterday that an attempt was to be made to get at Phar Lap and I intended to call at the Criminal Investigation Branch and ask for protection for the horse,' he said. 'I decided, however, to put it off until after the races today. From what happened this morning, the information was correct.'

Could that be right? The detectives agreed that if Telford had received such a threat yesterday, he would have told them about it this morning.

'I have no doubt that those responsible for the incident were financially interested and that they intended to kill the horse,' Davis continued. 'The trouble is the ante-post betting. No matter how low a man, it is strange that he would want to shoot a beautiful animal like Phar Lap.

'He will win the Melbourne Cup if he gets to the course.'

For the moment, the two detectives were just pleased Phar Lap had got to Derby Day in one piece. Woodcock and Joe Cripps had ridden in the float with the champion, with Stan Boyden driving and Senior Constable Davis in the passenger seat. Two policemen on motor cycles accompanied the float, and a third cyclist met them outside the course, to escort the party to their stall. There they were met by Brophy and Saker, Telford and David Davis, and a posse of plain-clothes officers, whose brief was to keep a close watch. Brophy spoke to Telford long enough to learn that just before the trainer left for Flemington he'd taken a phone call that all but flattened him. 'We missed him this time, but we'll get him,' a sinister voice had said slowly. 'He'll never start in the Cup.'

'Don't worry for now,' was all Brophy could say. 'Stay busy. They won't try to strike here on course.'

There was no way of knowing for sure that the bloke who made that call had also been in the Studebaker. It might have been some mug taking advantage of the situation. Brophy perused his copy of the *Herald* again, and then sought out his senior constable.

'Davis, tell us what you know about that James Creed.'

'He saw the car on his way to the track, sir.'

'Have you seen what he told his paper? He seems a lot keener to talk to them than to talk to you.'

Davis read the front page, quickly flicked inside, then returned to the front page. 'They've got a few things wrong here, sir,' he said. 'There seems to be some confusion as to who saw which number plate. It was Woodcock that noted the back number. I don't think there'd be any way in the world he was going to look back at that Studebaker straight after he and Phar Lap walked past it. And the paper might have got the newsboy's photo, but they couldn't get his Christian name right. His name is Ronald Taylor, not Norman.'

Brophy grunted. He didn't really care what the newsboy's name was.

'Creed says in here he saw the Studebaker outside the picture theatre at five past five,' Davis continued. 'He told me, "Between five and six o'clock". He was pretty vague, but I did speak to a good old bloke who says he saw the car charging down Augusta Street at precisely 5.05. Maybe Creed's just got his times wrong ...'

The senior constable waited politely for the dialogue to continue, but Brophy was now deep in thought, pondering exactly what the *Herald*'s track watcher might have been doing on Manchester Grove just nine hours ago. No aspect of Creed's job should have been more important than watching the Cup favourite. With Telford working Phar Lap at absolute first light, as early as 5am, Creed would have struggled to see the champ in action if at the same time he was strolling down a Caulfield side street.

Brophy was quickly coming to the conclusion that solving this crime was not going to be as simple as it first appeared. There was a lot of misinformation and intrigue about, and somewhere a 'marksman' who couldn't hit a 17-hands horse from 20 yards. Were they just trying to frighten the horse? Or the trainer? That's what the absence of pellet marks at the crime scene told him. If this was a warning, and Telford wasn't scared off, then next time, for sure, the gunman's aim would be true. So Brophy had to calculate exactly how many men he needed to protect the horse 24 hours a day for at least the next three days. That, he thought, would be a hell of a lot easier if he knew who or what he was up against. He had to scout the scene of the shooting for himself. That was essential, but it would have to wait, not least because the horses were on their way to the start for race two. There were also a number of racing people he'd like to talk to, on the course and off, some of whom, he was sure, could point him in the direction of the people who so badly wanted Phar Lap stopped. If there was any way he could, he wanted to bump into his boss, the Police Commissioner, whom he knew was in the Members' Reserve.

And before the day was out, he wanted to talk to James Creed.

CHAPTER FIVE

NOT THIS CUP
FAVOURITE

YOU CAN UNDERSTAND HOW it works. The shooting had already been a topic of most conversations on the trains and the trams, and in the car parks. As racegoers stood in queues, waiting to get into the track, 'Did you hear about Phar Lap?' was all anyone wanted to talk about. The latest version of events had to be true, just as the previous, completely different account, had been true.

The champion's arrival at the course effectively squashed the anguished rumour that he had been killed or injured. But what effect, if any, the shooting had had on the horse was still just guesswork.

'It's gotta hurt him, the shock of it all,' one self-proclaimed authority exclaimed. 'I know how I'd feel if someone took a shot at me.'

Down in the birdcage, the subject of debate among the stablehands already on course was the same, though hardly as furious as it was out in the public areas. From stall to stall, it was as if a code of silence had been put in place, and as soon as an unknown entered a conversation, the debate stopped. More than one trainer had told his staff to 'keep your mouths shut'. Leonard Searle had been advised to 'mind your own business' by his boss, so he stayed out of most discussions, happy to stand back and be struck by the fact that at least six or seven of the stable workers from Caulfield were now eyewitnesses to the assassination attempt. Manchester Grove at six in the morning hadn't been deserted after all. He heard one teenager from Joe Cripps' own stable quietly but excitedly tell how he had been within 100 yards of Woodcock on Manchester Grove.

'When I went past the theatre I noticed a big car like a Buick,' this young bloke whispered. 'I went over Glenhuntly Road, then about two or three minutes later they followed me and when they passed me they was blowing the horn. They followed Phar Lap up the first street on the right. There were two shots. They both missed.'

He went on to describe one of the assailants in extraordinary detail, something he could do because he'd seen him before at the races. 'I bet he's here today!' he said confidently.

The legend was growing by the minute.

SAM SULLIVAN HAD BEEN a bookmaker for 20 years, but he'd never seen it as bad as this. The problem, he'd explain to his mates, was that while the smart punters were still around, the onset of the bloody depression meant that too many of the mugs had vanished. All those poor people who used to bet in 10 shillings or £1 lots, not really caring if they won or lost — or, at least, that's how it appeared — were now worrying about every penny. Over the past two weeks, Sullivan tried every way he knew to get his balance sheet back in kilter, but everyone around him was suddenly a good judge. Things were getting worse. If Phar Lap won the Melbourne Cup, he'd be out of business.

How had it all come to this? Sullivan was from the old school. He did the percentages, knew his racing history and swore never to ride his luck because if you do, one day you'll get tipped off. He bet on the Melbourne meetings and specialised on the big doubles, especially the Caulfield Cup–Melbourne Cup double, and over the years that was one of his best earners. 'Sure, you might have to pay out plenty of cash in the end, but from the opening market in July to the first Tuesday in November you could skin a small fortune as the popular picks fell by the wayside,' he'd explain. 'If you kept a close eye on the odds, most years you could get yourself in a position where you couldn't get badly hurt. Occasionally the Cups could set you up for the whole year.'

If Sullivan had a problem, it was that sometimes he was a little too keen to back his judgement. Like many people, he had never been confident that Phar Lap would run in the Caulfield Cup, given that a win at Caulfield would mean a 10-pound penalty for the Melbourne Cup, and that was why, even as late as the end of August, the champ was only on the fourth line of betting. However, he had memories of 1926, when the great horse Manfred wasn't expected to run in the Caulfield Cup because a 10-pound penalty would take his Melbourne Cup weight to 10.1. However, in mid-September of that year a huge plunge was suddenly launched, which saw Manfred's price for the Caulfield race sink from 14–1 to as short as 5–4 on race day, and he won as comfortably as a champion should. Many observers thought him a special for the Melbourne Cup, but a leg injury suffered while winning the Melbourne Stakes prevented a start on the biggest day of all, and the bookies breathed again.

Making the 1930 picture more confusing for Sullivan was the fact that he didn't like Amounis in the Caulfield Cup either, not least because the horse would have to break the weight-carrying record to win. Amounis was an eight-year-old, and since the Caulfield Cup was first run as a handicap in the spring, in 1881, only two eight-year-olds had won the race. Amounis' record at a mile-and-a-half (the race distance) or longer was ordinary: two wins from 12 starts. In Sullivan's mind, the horse was at his best over a mile, perhaps 10 furlongs. He was also such a dud in the wet his owner Billy Pearson never backed him until the day of the race, just in case it rained.

Sullivan used weights, measures and history to cast doubt on Phar Lap's prospects in the Melbourne Cup, too. The big chestnut was being asked to lug a full nine pounds more than any four-year-old had ever carried to win the Cup. Back in 1889, the immortal Carbine had been beaten as a four-year-old carrying 10 stone, and as the time-honoured weight-for-age scale gave geldings three pounds, that meant Phar Lap was being asked to do more than what Carbine couldn't do. ('Weight for age' is the method of weight allocation for horses that makes allowances for the age and sex of the galloper and the time of the racing season. This means horses of different ages and either gender can compete in the same race under the most equal of conditions. Most of the best races are run under the weight-for-age scale, as is it said to allow the best horse to win.) Now Sam Sullivan wasn't sure if Phar Lap was better than Carbine, but his bookmaking logic told him that if someone wanted to back that proposition at the right price it was a bet worth accepting. He came to this conclusion cautiously, knowing that Phar Lap's performances over the previous 12 months had been freakish. In the year since his first big win, the 1929 Rosehill Guineas, the big red horse had won a succession of major races, often in record time, usually making hacks of his rivals. The only real blemish on his record was the 1929 Melbourne Cup, when he'd fought with his jockey for most of the journey and consequently been a sitting shot for Nightmarch at the end.

Interestingly, Phar Lap's record against Amounis was two wins each from four starts, and one of the younger horse's victories had been on a bog track. Amounis really was an old marvel, on the verge of breaking Gloaming's Australasian stakes-winning record, and the consensus was that the 1930 Caulfield Cup was a weaker race than 12 months before when Amounis, carrying 9.5, had beaten all but the Queenslander High Syce. So there was no reason to lengthen the price for the Amounis–Phar Lap double or either horse straight out to anything silly, but still Sullivan made sure his quote was the best on offer. From Sydney came an inquiry on behalf of Mrs Maude Vandenburg, Australia's best-known female punter. Mrs Vandenburg was as loyal to Amounis, her all-time favourite, as Sullivan was to his grandchildren, and the Melbourne bookie let her on, both straight out in the Caulfield Cup, and doubled with Phar Lap in the Melbourne Cup. This was around the start of October, just before Amounis won the October Stakes.

Mrs Vandenburg had become so well known that the *Truth*, published every Sunday in Sydney, grandly called her 'Madame X' or simply 'Sydney's lady punter'. At first glance, she might have been your grandmother, except that she wagered in thousands, and came to prominence after her husband, a bookmaker, collapsed and died while preparing to head out to the races in 1920. Her support for Amounis became almost legendary, and she'd cost one bookmaker, 'Gentleman' Jim Hackett, more than £20,000 at the spring carnival in 1929, after Hackett risked the gelding in the Cantala Stakes. The bookmaker's logic was impeccable: Amounis had been through a tough time running second in the Caulfield Cup, he was coming back from a mile-and-a-half to a mile in the Cantala, and that he was carrying a hefty top weight of 9.12. But Mrs Vandenburg knew her horse. She walked up to Hackett and asked for £7000 to £2000, to which the bookie reputedly replied, 'Madam, you can have it again if you like.' Which the lady punter did, and then she boldly challenged him once more. Only then did Hackett bring the odds into 3–1. Amounis romped home.

Mrs Vandenburg's bets on the Cups double in 1930, which she placed in the third week of September, signalled the start of a flood and Sullivan let them all on, mostly at 25–1, for as long as he dared. Later he read in the papers that the notorious Eric Connolly was mainly responsible. They were mostly little bets, but lots of them, from a posse of Connolly's mates, and when the bookie next pored over his betting sheets, he realised he'd overdone it. He was then disappointed to learn that because his fellow doubles bookmakers, both in Melbourne and interstate, also had some serious liabilities, he couldn't balance his ledger to some degree by backing the Amounis–Phar Lap double with them. It was common practice for bookmakers to accept bets and then 'lay off' some of the liabilities they'd incurred by backing the same horse or horses, on a smaller scale, with other bookies. In this instance, Sullivan even tried a few of the off-course, unlicensed SP (starting price) bookmakers he might have trusted, but they'd also been bitten. Then Nightmarch was scratched, then Phar Lap. Sam Sullivan was out on a limb, never a good place for a bookmaker to be.

If he needed a friend, he could have found one in Sydney. David Macfarlane 'Andy' Kerr was a colourful racing identity who was known far and wide as 'The Coogee Bunyip'. As a bookmaker, he was a showman who'd bet a punter down on his luck £100 to a cigarette, or maybe a hundred to absolutely nothing at all. Everything was about attracting business. During a slow period in late September 1930, Kerr came up with the idea of offering a double of £500 for the Caulfield and Melbourne Cups for anyone who could lodge a credit of £10, that double being the combination of the punter's choice. Connolly heard about the scheme, and got as many of his associates as he could find to sign up, all of them taking the damned Amounis–Phar Lap double. When Kerr did the sums after the Caulfield Cup he realised that if the double came true, he was broke.

Sullivan thought back to happier spring carnivals, like 1921, when the 16–1 hope Sister Olive, a three-year-old filly, won the Melbourne Cup with the heavily backed favourite Eurythmic last after a chequered run. Another 16–1 pop, Violoncello, had won the Caulfield Cup, and you could have got any old price that double. No one did.

WHEN JACK BROPHY WANDERED over to talk to Sullivan not long before race two on Derby Day, he lost no time asking after 'Mr Wren'. It was common knowledge that John Wren was one of Sullivan's regular clients, so it made sense to the bookmaker that Brophy would raise Wren's name, given that the businessman had been mentioned in one or two conversations about the shooting, as though he might have been behind it. Sullivan knew that was absurd and was happy to say so.

Born in 1871, John Wren was a hero around Collingwood, a working-class suburb most renowned for its football club and as the site of the now defunct but once thriving betting shop — Wren's famous 'tote'. This self-made man had become extremely wealthy on the back of this illegal operation and many other sharp entrepreneurial ventures into the worlds of sport and entertainment, and while most of his fortune went into buying him respectability, part of it went into trying to own a Melbourne Cup winner.

Many in the Establishment despised him and often whispered his name if something untoward occurred in the endeavour they liked to call 'The Sport of Kings'. By the 1920s, the underworld of unlicensed gambling was seedy and totally corrupted, and some people were inclined to blame Wren for that, on the extremely tenuous basis that he'd helped start it all. When Kentle, owned by no less than the Chairman of the VRC, Mr LKS Mackinnon, was nobbled in the lead-up to the Grand National Steeplechase in July 1930, a couple of committeemen, including Mackinnon himself, were quoted in the press as saying it was the work of a 'doping gang'. This claim was sensationalised in the popular press, and privately a couple of fingers were pointed at Wren, which was ridiculous — he might have been involved in illegal activity of a different kind back in the days of his tote, but that was more than 20 years ago. That his name was being raised again now was as good an indicator as any that no one in high places knew exactly what was going on.

Mr Wren had a horse in the 1930 Melbourne Cup, the outsider Muratti. Sam Sullivan fully expected Mr Wren to back his horse, and he'd be happy accommodate him, but he knew, too, that unless the wager was of world-record proportions, Muratti was the least of his worries. He explained that to Mr Brophy, but the detective appeared distracted, apparently more concerned with getting into the grandstand to watch the next race. Brophy would let Saker do most of the racecourse investigations, which made sense given his partner's many contacts around the track. One day recently, Harold had told him that the way the force was going his ultimate ambition was to become a stipendiary steward, one of that elite crew employed by the VRC, men who wear unfashionable felt hats and make or break careers with their interpretation of what goes on in 'questionable' races.

'I'll be back in a while, Sam,' Brophy said. 'I don't really want to hear about how bad you're going. But I do need to find out what you know about Phar Lap.'

WHEN SULLIVAN HEARD THAT Phar Lap had been shot, it didn't occur to him that a member of the bookmaking fraternity at Flemington might have done it. His first reaction, like a number of other people, was to blame the mob who'd got at Kentle back in July, and nobbled the easing second favourite, Wise Force, with cocaine before the October Stakes at Flemington. The rumours about a 'doping gang' terrorising racing had been so strong they had to be right. When news broke, a few hours after the Phar Lap shooting, that Cragford, which started second favourite in the Caulfield Cup, had died, blame was again quickly put on the as yet unidentified dopers. However, as one of Sullivan's clerks pointed out, this gang was supposed to be ruthless; if they were shooting to kill, they'd kill.

Sullivan could think of plenty of instances of punters and betting syndicates being up to no good in recent years, but he honestly couldn't name one licensed Melbourne bookie who he believed would go as far as to kill a horse, especially a great horse like Phar Lap. And he believed this knowing that bookies could be as hard-nosed as anyone. One of his favourite Cup yarns concerned 1876, when the SS *City of Melbourne* sailed for Melbourne with 12 classy thoroughbreds aboard, among them the ruling Cup favourite. South of Jervis Bay, on the NSW south coast, a storm hit, but for too long Captain Paddle, the ship's skipper, refused to take shelter. Only one horse survived — a classy unnamed colt that had already won the AJC Derby and which was later given the rather apt title of 'Robinson Crusoe' — and Captain Paddle was condemned by all but the Melbourne bookmakers, who instead presented him with a financial reward as a token of their appreciation for the role he played in the catastrophe.

Of course, times had changed since then. Sullivan figured that it had to be the SPs who'd done the shooting, or who got someone to do it on their behalf. But then, as soon as he put up his stand for Derby Day, he saw a couple of his staff talking to other bookie's clerks and started to realise that in some people's eyes he was a serious suspect. Bloody hell, was the word that strong about his lack of funds? No wonder Mr Brophy wanted a chat.

Sullivan had seen some amazing racing schemes over the years, and always tried to work them to his advantage if he could. If a bookie got some good mail about a horse 'going slow', which happened from time to time, he didn't call the cops or the stewards, he tried to make a quid out of the information. That's not cheating, just common sense. Same as if you heard a rumour that a horse was injured, or had been going no good on the training track. You don't spread the word, just make something else favourite and let the punters on. What if you had heard that someone had tried to shoot the Cup favourite? Would you go to the authorities? Probably not, but you would be tempted to ease his price a little.

Not this Cup favourite. 'If he's still alive at Tuesday lunchtime,' Sullivan muttered to one punter who made an inquiry, 'he'll probably be odds on.' Which was unbelievable. No horse had ever started odds on in a Melbourne Cup.

The bookmaker had to find out all he could, and after La Justice got the money by three-quarters of a length in race two — at 20-1, thank you very much — he left his clerks to count the winnings and dashed off to find some friends who'd know for sure if something was happening. But the weird thing was that nobody knew anything. Everyone had a theory, but whereas in the good old days he would have found out all he needed to know, on this Derby Day everyone was guessing. By the time Sullivan returned to put up a market for race three, the Melbourne Stakes, he'd come to the conclusion that whoever was responsible for the shooting of Phar Lap, they were not from the world of racing. Which made the attack much more sinister, as if his second home was being overtaken by a conspiratorial force. Even Sam Sullivan was seeing Chicago gangsters in the shadows.

JACK BROPHY, MEANWHILE, WAS supervising Phar Lap's transfer from the birdcage to the mounting yard. The champion hardly had time to adjust to his stall and he was being guarded by no less than 10 plain-clothes policemen. It was amazing to watch the scene in and around his stall, with Telford flustered by the lack of time he had to get his charge ready, young Woodcock too polite to do anything but get ordered about, and everywhere there were men, young and old, looking for trouble, the brims of their trilby hats pulled hard over their eyes. Maybe one or two were gangsters, searching for an opening? Or so it seemed. The only one unperturbed by the mood was the great horse. Occasionally, his chestnut head looked out of his stall and over the turmoil around him; he was like a king above his subjects.

As Phar Lap walked up the chase from the birdcage, the crowd was six or seven deep, but so heavy was the police guard it was hard for the punters to get too good a look at him. As soon as he was in the mounting yard, the clerk of the course kept his white horse between the crowd and the champion, and quickly as they could, Jim Pike was legged aboard. Controversially, the VRC

Committee had ruled that the police weren't allowed onto the track, and the big horse suddenly looked very lonely as he cantered around to the 10-furlongs start. It seemed Mackinnon and his cronies on the committee wanted to assert their authority, and this was the only way they could.

With the horses around at the barrier, Brophy relaxed, if only for an instant. Suddenly, he felt a hand on his shoulder, and trying not to appear startled, spun around as quickly as he dared.

'Busy day, Detective-Sergeant?'

Jack Brophy found himself face-to-face with a war hero: Brigadier-General Thomas Blamey, Chief Commissioner of the Victoria Police.

CHAPTER SIX

SECRECY IS THE KEY

GENERAL BLAMEY'S NAME HAD first come to public attention during the Gallipoli campaign of 1915. As the intelligence officer at the First Australian Division headquarters, he helped plan the operation that began on April 25 and went ashore within hours of the first landing. Between May and July he was often involved in front-line action, a prelude to his time on the Western Front, where he made his reputation and rose to become Chief of Staff of the Australian Corps, commanded by Lieutenant-General Sir John Monash. After the war, he spent two years as the Australian Army's representative in London before returning to Melbourne to become Victoria's 10th Police Commissioner.

When it came to racing, it was said Blamey had three ambitions: to own a good horse, become a VRC Committeeman and have a major race named after him. At this point in his life, however, he was yet to savour the joys of ownership and was not even a member of the club, though he was happy to accept free entrance tickets whenever he needed them. While his military service record was highly regarded, he was hardly a popular figure in the community, a man who demanded the highest standards from others while occasionally finding himself in awkward situations. This was never more true than in his first year as police chief, when his identification badge was used by someone to dodge arrest in a Fitzroy brothel. The Commissioner claimed the badge had been lost, which might have been true, and when the matter was raised in the papers and in parliament some of the mud stuck.

At the same time, such was his military record, his appointment by the ruling conservative government had been enough to stifle calls for a public inquiry into police corruption. Commissioner Blamey took on the Victorian Police Association, which he saw as the embodiment of the communist forces that threatened to take over unless the elite asserted its authority. A positive profile in Keith Murdoch's magazine *Table Talk* in October 1926 happily tagged him a fascist and featured a cartoon of the Commissioner complete with a backdrop of policemen with batons raised, drawn in the shape of a swastika. Such were the times. Blamey used the police to repel protesting members of the unemployed as the depression took hold, a policy encapsulated in one notorious incident in 1928, when police protecting strikebreakers used their guns against a group of stevedores, wounding four people, one seriously. He was most unhappy that the unemployed were taking to the streets as a way of demonstrating against their misfortune, and deplored the fact that there was no law in place to prohibit street marches. There were rumours about that he issued a direction to his officers that unemployed people causing a breach of the peace could be hit over the head with batons. 'There is little room for discretion in dealing with mobs which, under the guise of sympathy for the unemployed, are bent upon wanton destruction and violence,' he was quoted as saying. 'Unbalanced and subversive elements in the community which seize upon every opportunity to flout the law are at present deserving of even less sympathy than usual.' Such comments, when mixed with the image of gangsters such as Squizzy Taylor and Snowy Cutmore blasting each other to death, added to the picture of a city on the verge of being out of control. Yet Blamey was hardly one-dimensional. He had also established a Police Provident Fund to support members struggling in difficult times.

The Commissioner had many acquaintances but few friends, being one of those people you always suspected was being matey for a reason. He was prone to play people off against each other, and recognised, as a military officer and as Police Commissioner, that if he wanted to get his way there were political games to be played. He understood this better than virtually anyone else in the Army, and better than most left-wing activists as well. However, Blamey was not always so clever in his battles with the media. Newspaper editors tend to have longer memories than politicians, and when he closed the press room at the CIB's Russell Street headquarters and tried to stop his officers leaking information to reporters, cutting off a lifeline the scribes relied on, he made some enemies.

Brophy was one man who'd been happy to oblige when Blamey asked his detectives to stop leaking to the press. So there was a certain irony in him now being in charge of an investigation that would inevitably be a major story over the next few days, probably the next few weeks. Whichever way you looked at it, this was a story the headline writers could have some fun with. Brophy's *modus operandi* had always been to avoid being quoted if he could help it. It was Senior Constable Davis who had helped the reporters this morning, and Detective Saker who had given a couple of brief interviews here at the course, so Blamey was getting just about exclusive access when Brophy admitted to him that he had little to go on.

'We asked for the two car plate numbers to be checked,' he said, as someone nearby shouted that the horses were moving in. 'But to be honest, I doubt they'll lead to anything. They were written in chalk or paint, almost certainly phony.'

'Up in the committee room, they're blaming it on the SP bookmakers,' Blamey replied. 'I don't think they'd be too upset if you could prove that was true.'

Brophy stopped for a moment, trying to see from Blamey's face if that was an order. Mr Mackinnon had been leading a push for the government to allow a totalisator to be established at Flemington, and Blamey knew from his connections in high places that passing the Bill approving such an innovation was a mere formality, even though it wouldn't be universally popular. One of the VRC's arguments was that too much racing revenue was being lost to the SPs, and an official tote that lured people to the track would help reverse that trend, but they also knew that the 'wowsers' didn't agree with them, so there was a public relations battle to be won. Besmirching the SPs in any way possible had to be a good thing.

'It could easily be the bookies. They've got a motive, with all the shenanigans over the Cups double,' Brophy said. 'But the few people I've spoken to here on course either can't or won't tell me anything about it.'

The term 'SP bookie' actually covered a broad group of various types, ranging from small fry who accepted bets at the local pub to much larger operations most likely backed by shadowy 'underworld' figures. Both Brophy and Blamey knew that while it was all very well to say the underworld was responsible for the shooting, in Melbourne these days the underworld was a bloody big place. People making accusations really needed to be a bit more specific.

At that moment, the five-horse field jumped in the Melbourne Stakes, and the policemen's attention turned to the race. This was the VRC's principal weight-for-age middle-distance event, which meant Phar Lap carried three pounds less than Amounis and Donald, had the same weight as Carradale, but gave 13 pounds to the three-year-old Tregilla. As he always was in WFA races, Phar Lap started a pronounced odds-on favourite, the best price available being 6–1 on. He missed the start slightly, but Pike bustled him forward and for maybe a furlong Phar Lap, Amounis and Mackinnon's horse Carradale fought for the lead. After that the champ took charge, his advantage down the back being two lengths from Amounis, then Donald, Carradale and Tregilla, and by the final turn, two-and-a-quarter furlongs from home, he was four lengths clear and cruising. Tregilla chased vainly all the way down the straight, putting in a superb Cup trial, while Amounis was grossly disappointing, the final margin being three lengths between first and second, and four between second and third. The big surprise was the time — just three-quarters of a second outside the course record, yet the winner had missed the start and never been pressed. This was Phar Lap's seventh straight victory, and his 20th success from his last 23 starts (one second, two thirds) dating back to September 1929. Carradale was a full 10 lengths behind the placegetters, and as soon as he got down to the mounting yard from his premium vantage point in the stands, the VRC Chairman was announcing to anyone who'd listen that straight after the Cup the damn horse would be going into the sales ring.

Harry Telford watched intently as Pike brought Phar Lap back, searching for any sign that something might have gone wrong in the run. But as a crucial trial before the biggest event of his life, the race had been perfect. As Telford watched Woodcock parade the horse around the mounting yard, he went back over to Mr Guy Raymond, the owner of the famous St Albans Stud at Geelong, south-west of Melbourne, to resume a very serious conversation the two had been engaged in before the jump. And before too long, the two discussions merged into one: Blamey and Brophy, Telford and Raymond.

ST ALBANS STUD HAD PRODUCED no fewer than five Melbourne Cup winners: Briseis (1876), Auraria (1895), Newhaven (1896), Merriwee (1899) and Revenue (1901). Another, Don Juan, which survived a mild heart attack a few days before winning in 1873, was trained on the property by the stud's founder, Mr James Wilson. During the 1890s, the property was owned by Mr WR Wilson (no relation to James), who in the annals of Cup history must go down as one of the unluckiest of owners. His ambition was to lead in the winner, but while St Albans bred three Cup victors while he was in charge, and a remarkable first, second, third and fifth in 1895, Mr Wilson himself couldn't take a trick.

His first good galloper was the colt Strathmore, which finished third in the Cup in 1891. Two years later, Wilson's VRC Derby winner Carnage appeared to have the big race won until worn down by the 40-1 pop Tarcoola, and then in 1894 Nada was caught up in a scrimmage on the home turn before just failing to run down Patron and Devon. In 1895, Wilson, who was battling ill-health, decided to dispose of St Albans and its bloodstock through a lottery involving 125,000 £1 tickets, but at the last minute he had a change of heart and bought the several thousand remaining tickets. After the draw, he set about buying back some of the prestigious lots he did not win, among them the stud itself and a classy Carbine colt named Wallace, which went on to claim that year's VRC Derby but ran poorly in the Cup.

Mr Wilson was again a bridesmaid in 1897, when Aurum ran third, carrying 14 pounds over weight for age. Soon after, this great colt was sold to the English actress Lily Langtry, she of Edward VII fame, but a traumatic voyage to Britain did him no favours, and he never raced and was a failure at stud. The horse that ran second in his Cup was a tough ugly stayer called The Grafter, which became available for sale before the 1898 race. However, his original owner, Mr William Forrester of Warwick Farm, west of Sydney, also had The Chief in the Cup, which concerned Wilson. 'If I buy The Grafter,' he said, 'can you guarantee that The Chief will not beat him?'

Forrester could not do so — racing's not like that — so Wilson vetoed the deal. 'I can't buy him,' he explained. 'If I do and The Chief wins, people will put me down as a fool and you as a rogue.'

So Forrester had two Cup runners, and of course The Grafter won, with The Chief seventh. Wilson was left with his pride and regrets. Within two years, the St Albans owner was dead, and at a subsequent dispersal sale a four-year-old gelding named Revenue went for 725 guineas. Set for the 1901 Cup, he romped in as a 7–4 favourite, which remained the shortest price a winner had ever started in Melbourne Cup history. It was just another record Phar Lap would have to beat if he was to win on Tuesday.

Guy Raymond had won the Military Cross in France as a lieutenant in the AIF's 12th Field Artillery Brigade before rising to the rank of captain. He acquired St Albans in 1926, hoping to return the property to its glory days after a quarter of a century of neglect. Six days before the 1930 Victoria Derby, he and his partner, Hugh Ranken, had staged an open day, and it was during that event that he first met Telford, and where he said to Phar Lap's trainer, 'If there is anything I can do, please do not hesitate to let me know.' The offer was about to be taken up; all they needed was the police's approval. Telford was happy for Raymond to do the talking.

'General Blamey, Mr Telford and I have come up with a strategy,' the stud owner began. 'He is keen to get his horse away from Caulfield and I am happy to help. With your permission, tonight I would like to get Phar Lap to St Albans.'

Blamey looked at Brophy, who shook his head. 'Captain, this is Detective-Sergeant Brophy. I am not sure he thinks that is such a good idea.'

'Mr Raymond,' Brophy began. 'We don't really know what we're dealing with. I think it would be harder to protect the horse in the country than it will be where he is.'

'Detective-Sergeant, I am sure you are right,' Raymond replied quietly. 'But only if the hoodlums know he is there. What we are suggesting is that we move him in the middle of the night, and tell as few people as practical where he is going. If needs be, I can arrange for him to gallop in private at Geelong. Telford can even rug up one of his other horses at Caulfield to look like him, to make it look as if it is business as usual.'

Brophy was about to point out that after missing out this morning there was every chance the gunmen would be watching Cripps' stables night and day, and that Telford and Raymond might be playing into their hands. He had visions of the float being run off the road on the Melbourne–Geelong highway, or a sniper firing away in the early morning at a deserted Geelong racecourse. However, his boss interrupted.

'I think it is an excellent plan,' Blamey said. 'Secrecy is the key. Mr Telford, rest assured Detective-Sergeant Brophy will ensure that we do all we can to help.'

With that, the Chief Commissioner was off back to the committee room. Gwyn Jones, the racing correspondent for the *Herald*, who had been patiently waiting for the four men to complete their discussion, quickly slipped into Blamey's place in the conversation. Inevitably, Jones was keen for a quiet word with the trainer of the Cup favourite, but Telford wanted to get his horse out of here. Instead, Brophy took the opportunity to ask the journalist how it might be possible to get in touch with James Creed.

Jones told him he didn't think 'Jim' had come to the course. Creed was up early this morning, and though he might be here — 'just having a bet and catching up with some mates' — the best place to find him would be in the infield of Caulfield racecourse at dawn. 'Maybe you could catch him at home, in Malvolio Street, not far from where Phar Lap is staying,' Jones added. 'Number five, I think.'

'What do you know about the shooting?' was Brophy's next question.

'Only what I've heard at the track,' Jones replied. 'Some off-course bookies are in way too deep over the double. Nothing else was going to beat Phar Lap, so they had to do it themselves.'

'Not the licensed boys?' Brophy asked.

'Not what I've heard. I'm sure you've heard the same thing. It's not impossible, but I don't think so. They were rogues 50 years ago, but not now.'

'It was a nice front page your paper did this afternoon,' Brophy changed tack again. 'I suppose you'll have another go on Monday.'

'I guess they will, I just do the races,' Jones replied. 'Trouble is, all the other papers would have caught up by Monday morning. Hopefully, you blokes will make an arrest on Monday about 10.30, 11, and we can scoop everyone all over again. Otherwise, we'll just have to put our Cup tip on page one, and everyone knows what that's going to be.'

'So he is unbeatable?'

'I think so, he's an unbelievable horse. The way he wins so easily, and so often. Though I guess you can mount a case against him. That Tregilla ran a nice race today, and he meets him way better at the weights. If you can find a bookie who still does weights and measures, you'll find a bloke who'll tell you Phar Lap can't win. Maybe Veilmond or Balloon King will run a big race in the Derby, and a couple of the horses in the Hotham are pretty good stayers. And, you know, detective, he got ...'

'Detective-Sergeant.'

'Detective-Sergeant. You know, Phar Lap got beat in the Cup last year. He wouldn't settle, didn't seem to run out the two mile. He wouldn't be the first champion that couldn't stay two mile at Flemington.'

'And not many have done the Melbourne Stakes–Cup double.'

'That's right. Only two, I believe. And Pike's never won the Cup. It's a bogy race for some jockeys, you know. Look at Frank Dempsey, with Billy Duncan the best jockey in Victoria in my opinion, ridden 10 or 11 Cups, horses like Eurythmic and Manfred, but never won it. Maybe Pike's the same. And I know Phar Lap didn't show it today, but there's all this fracas about the shooting. I bet you blokes will be all over him for the next three days. It's got to hurt him, hasn't it? He'll start odds-on on Tuesday, but that's only because the bookies are facing a big payout on him. I don't think he should be odds on, not with all that's happening.'

'I'd better be going and checking on my horse,' Brophy said. He thanked Jones for his time, asked him to tell James Creed if he saw him that the police would like a chat.

For the experienced detective, Creed had become a person of real interest. If they couldn't dig any information out of the racetrack — and from what he was finding and his partner was soon telling him, that was what was happening — then the *Herald*'s Caulfield track watcher represented perhaps his best hope. He'd apparently walked past the Studebaker before it took off after Phar Lap. With Woodcock and the paperboy unable to identify the driver or the gunmen, Creed was the one man left 'at the scene' who might be able to do so. Brophy also needed to clarify exactly when Creed saw the vehicle parked outside the picture theatre. He couldn't have been walking past at the same time Leonard Searle was dodging the car as it careered down Augusta Road, but that's what seems to have happened if you believed what Searle told Senior Constable Davis and what Creed said to the *Herald*.

Brophy returned to the birdcage to check on Phar Lap, and found that his men had done a superb job and that Telford was just about ready to go. Brophy had agreed with Guy Raymond and now confirmed with the trainer that they'd meet later at Joe Cripps' place to finalise details of the clandestine transfer to Geelong. Meanwhile, while those policemen in their trilbies kept the keen and curious as far away as they could, the crowd around the stall was as big as it had ever been, even though the Victoria Derby was only 15 minutes away. Such was power of the big red horse.

As far as these punters were concerned, the Cup was as good as won. Jack Brophy knew that there still a very long way to go.

CHAPTER SEVEN

THE VICTORIA DERBY

'BATTLING' BILLY TINDALL PUNTED for a living, so he knew there was no value in 'what might have beens'. Still, he couldn't help thinking he was the unluckiest man alive. He remembered the day at Randwick only too well, when he fronted Harry Telford just after an ungainly, unknown two-year-old called Phar Lap had put in an impressive gallop. 'Harry, I'll give you every horse in my stable for him,' Tindall had said. He was fair dinkum, too, but Telford ignored him.

That was April 1929. No one thought of Billy as unlucky back then, but as Phar Lap developed into a champion he couldn't help but think that if he'd just been more assertive, Harry might have blinked. After all, it wasn't like he was rolling in cash. Billy himself was well established in Sydney town as a fearless punter and canny owner-trainer, a character who fitted perfectly in the pages of the *Truth*, which loved to excitedly tell its readers of the latest goings-on from the betting ring. He was a man rarely seen without a black Stetson sitting rakishly on his head, who limited himself to training horses he owned, the logic being that if you do that, 'You don't have to make plans to suit anyone but yourself.' Perhaps his greatest moment had come one afternoon at the Moorefield races, after he lost £800 on the first two races, leaving him with a shilling less than a quid in loose change. Undaunted, he found a gatekeeper who'd let him out and then back onto the course, sold his racebook to a late arrival for a shilling, and then went back to turn one pound into five thousand.

By the start of 1930, Billy had almost got over his Phar Lap disappointment. Then the Australian Jockey Club (AJC) stewards disqualified him for 12 months after an inquiry into the running of one of his horses, a nag called Shankara, in a race at Warwick Farm. This really was a major setback, because it meant he had to offload all his stable, which he did reluctantly, especially in the case of an unraced two-year-old named Tregilla that he really thought might develop into something. Which, of course, is exactly what he did, emulating Phar Lap by winning the AJC Derby, Sydney's equivalent of the Victoria Derby. Originally, the ownership of the colt had been transferred to the wife of trainer Cecil Battye, which was fine in NSW, where wives of trainers were permitted to own horses, but quirkily unacceptable in Victoria and South Australia. Consequently, Tregilla's nomination for the Victoria Derby, required long before the race was run, was rejected and the ownership had to be further reassigned to Mr Battye before the VRC would accept the colt's entry for the Melbourne Cup. This was why Tregilla ran in the Melbourne Stakes on Derby Day, and not in the Derby.

Having enthusiastically chased Phar Lap home in the Cox Plate and then the Melbourne Stakes, Tregilla was now a firm second favourite for the Cup. He'd be meeting the champion 20 pounds better on their Melbourne Stakes weights for being beaten three lengths, which was a big advantage, even allowing for the fact that Pike had taken a long look over his shoulder as he cruised past the winning post, suggesting he had plenty in hand. After the Cox Plate the week before, Tregilla's jockey Ted Bartle had said, 'Coming to the turn, I didn't think he would get a place, but when I gave him a flick with the whip he went on in great style. He'll keep Phar Lap going at the finish of the Cup.' That's great news, thought Battling Billy Tindall. He knew his best ever chance of winning a Melbourne Cup had been cruelly taken away from him, that he'd been unlucky. A punter without confidence is like a knight without armour. Life would never be the same.

WITH TREGILLA OUT OF the Victoria Derby, the race now looked set up for Veilmond. Owned by another colourful Sydney racing identity, Ned Moss, Veilmond was only small, with a prominent white blaze, and gradually he'd built a reputation as one of those horses that too often found a way not to win. He'd looked a likely stayer when second to The Doctor's Orders in the AJC's principal two-year-old race, the Sires Produce Stakes, on Easter Saturday 1930, and six months later was knocked over in the first major staying test for three-year-olds, the Rosehill Guineas, a controversial encounter won by Balloon King from Tregilla. Afterwards, Veilmond's connections alleged that their colt had been 'deliberately dealt with'. In the AJC Derby, Veilmond ran second after striking trouble at the nine furlongs and again at the five, but Tregilla was also impeded, so the pundits were unsure as to which was the superior colt, but certainly Mr and Mrs Battye's galloper looked the better of the two behind Phar Lap in the Cox Plate.

Ned Moss' association with the track started when he worked as a newsboy, selling papers outside the Sydney racecourses. From there, he advanced to hawking racebooks, and such was his sunny nature a number of high-profile racing figures took a liking to him. Among them was trainer Frank McGrath, who one day asked the youngster to help him put some money on a horse called Stormy. Ned was thrilled to help, and sharp, too, and he invested not just Mr McGrath's money but all of his own plus the day's takings from the sale of racebooks. Stormy saluted, and Ned Moss' career as a professional punter had begun.

By 1920, Ned was a successful businessman, able to back the Cups double of the great Eurythmic and his three-year-old, Erasmus, to win £100,000. Eurythmic, owned by the wealthy Perth pastoralist and now chairman of the WA Turf Club, Mr Ernest Lee Steere (who had Second Wind engaged in the 1930 Cup), was the first great horse to emerge from Western Australia and he won famously at Caulfield. Then, on Cup Day, Erasmus shot clear in the straight and looked home until the mighty Poitrel emerged from the pack to run him down. Afterwards, Ned refused to be disappointed, telling friends, 'I would have been ashamed if my lightweight had taken the race off a champion like Poitrel with his 10 stone. I'm glad the best horse won.' What he didn't reveal at the time was that he'd also backed the topweight to win £4000, which helped soothe the blow.

Moss' prime ambition was to win a Derby at Randwick or Flemington, and twice in the 1920s, with Vaals in 1925 and Sion two years later, he had a three-year-old good enough to run a place in the Rosehill Guineas. However, neither was up to the tougher staying tests of the Derbies. Veilmond seemed to be his best chance, especially considering that most observers thought the 1930 race was one of the weakest on record. 'Veilmond will have to win decisively in order to continue to enter into Cup calculations' was the view of the *Arrow's* correspondent.

Ned had bought Veilmond on one of his rare visits to New Zealand. In January 1929 he took a liking to a colt by Limond out of a mare called Veil that was to be offered at the yearling sales, not knowing that Mr Percy Miller, part-owner of the famed Kia Ora stud, a gentleman from one of Australia's most renowned racing families, was also intending to bid. But Miller organised a pre-sale inspection, and a terse report came back: 'Veil colt too small.' Instead of having one of Australia's biggest studs up against him, Ned was on his own, and soon the colt was in the stables of George Price and showing plenty of promise.

A few years earlier, Percy Miller and his brother Bob had been left with five young horses that needed trainers. Two men, Price and Peter Riddle, were called up, and told that one would get to train three of the horses, the other man, two. Ned's job was to toss the coin, to see who would get first pick. Price called correctly, took his turn, then Riddle, Price again, Riddle again, and Price was stuck with as ungainly a colt as you could find, one that had been rejected with hardly a bid at two yearling sales. The plan was to put him into work as soon as possible, to discover if he had any ability at all, and then to get rid of him when he confirmed he was no good. But Price, a canny New Zealand-born horseman who for good reason was Ned's favourite trainer, worked hard on the little horse, massaging him regularly to 'build him up'. Actually he wasn't too bad, as tough as asphalt, and Bob Miller would later describe Price as 'the miracle man'. The colt was Windbag, winner of the 1925 Melbourne Cup.

BALLOON KING, SECOND FAVOURITE for the 1930 Victoria Derby, had finished four lengths behind Tregilla and Veilmond at Randwick, and few thought him likely to turn the tables here. In the racebook, his ownership was listed as 'the estate of the late

J.A. Brown', which meant he was the last really good horse to race in Mr Brown's very familiar colours of pale blue, yellow sleeves, black cap. John Brown had been one of the real stalwarts of Australian coal mining since the 1880s and the Australian turf for more than 30 years before his death eight months before the 1930 spring carnival. Born in 1851 at Four Mile Creek, near Morpeth in the Hunter Valley, a little way west of Newcastle and 100 miles north of Sydney, he had taken over the family mining company, 'J. & A. Brown' from his father and turned it into a colossus, after starting in the firm's head office in Newcastle as a 14-year-old clerk. He served as a deckhand on one of the firm's tugboats, spent time down the mines, worked in sales, landed some lucrative contracts to supply coal to various parts of the world, and studied mining techniques in Britain and America, all before he took over the top job. In 1881 he married in Scotland but sadly his wife died within eight months, leaving a bitterness in his character that he never really lost. Back home, the tragedy may have played a part in further sharpening his business edge, because for the best part of the next half-century even his most grandiose plans came to fruition.

In the 1890s, Brown began to develop his horse-racing and thoroughbred-breeding interests. Racing under the pseudonym of 'Mr J. Baron', he had his first big-race success with Superb in the 1897 Doncaster Handicap at Randwick, and five years later a horse he imported, Sir Foote, won the Futurity Stakes and Newmarket Handicap in Melbourne. At stud, Sir Foote sired two of Brown's greatest horses, Prince Foote and Duke Foote. The latter was beaten as a 6–4 favourite in the Cup of 1912, and no horse started at a shorter price in the Cup until the three-year-old Phar Lap ran third at even money.

The winner of that 1912 Cup was Piastre, owned by Mr Brown's brother William. The previous year, the two had bet each other a new top hat about which of their horses would finish in front of the other, but both finished so far behind the winner, The Parisian, that a friendly family dispute arose as to which horse was actually first home. Consequently, for 1912 the stakes were increased to a total new outfit — hat, suit, shoes, socks, handkerchief, underwear — with a proviso added that at least one horse had to run a place.

Another of Brown's better gallopers was Richmond Main, named after Brown's biggest colliery, which dead-heated with Artilleryman in the 1919 AJC Derby, beat that colt by half a length in the Victoria Derby but then had the tables well and truly turned in the Melbourne Cup. At the time, most people thought the Cup winner was the better three-year-old, and subsequent tragic events suggested this was almost certainly correct. Artilleryman's connections had been concerned about his health during that spring carnival, and their worst fears were realised the following year when the colt's condition deteriorated and he quickly succumbed to cancer. He had won the Cup decisively despite a severe handicap.

To many in the mining and racing industries, Brown was an imposing figure, respected but not liked. Many saw him as dictatorial, and some believed Duke Foote's inexplicable Cup defeat (the *Age* had suggested beforehand that the race would be a 'benefit' for the favourite) was caused by the owner overruling the trainer's pre-race plans by insisting he run in the Melbourne Stakes.

But three years earlier, after Prince Foote's emphatic victory, Brown was talking with Frank McGrath when he suddenly said, 'You've won the Cup for me, what can I do for you?'

'You can make a gift to charity in the Prince's name,' McGrath replied.

Brown was taken aback. 'What? Nothing for yourself?'

'It'll do us both some good,' McGrath quipped.

And maybe it did. Every year for the next 20 years, until the coal miner's death, a considerable sum was donated to a worthy cause based in the Newcastle region. John Brown was buried at East Maitland in March 1930, in the same cemetery as the great boxer Les Darcy, after a funeral procession watched in bare-headed silence by bosses, miners, members of the racing fraternity and hundreds of grieving Novocastrians.

THE BIGGEST FACTOR IN Balloon King's favour in the Victoria Derby was that he would be ridden by Jim Pike, who was gunning for his third consecutive win in the race, after successes on Strephon and Phar Lap. To this point, Pike had not really been caught up in the furore over the Phar Lap shooting, as far as police protection and assassination attempts were concerned, but he soon would be. All he knew had come from the phone call from Telford he'd taken first thing this morning, telling him to be careful, and the incessant gossip he'd heard in the jockeys' room from the moment he arrived at the track. Until now, he'd dismissed the odd threatening call as coming from a crank, and it hardly occurred to him that as Phar Lap's rider he was something of a target himself. After all, he reasoned, if they knocked him over, there were plenty of other good jockeys keen for the ride.

For the moment, he could focus on 'his' race: the Victoria Derby. Back in 1910, it had been his first big win, as an 18-year-old apprentice on a stayer called Beverage, which was trained by his master, Bill Kelso, and was blind in its right eye. Three years later, now a fully fledged jockey, Pike won it again, on Beragoon, and though he fought a constant battle with weight that restricted his opportunities to some degree, such was his class he still forged a reputation as just about Australia's finest all-round rider. He was tall for a jockey, and had a constantly gaunt look that made him appear much older than he was and reflected too many lonely hours in the steam room. He was also a terrible punter and an honest man, a strange mix in the racing game, and stories were legion of him producing masterly rides that cost him money because he'd backed one of the beaten brigade. In 1928, Statesman won the Melbourne Cup for Kelso, but was ridden by another great jockey, Jim Munro, because Pike couldn't get down to eight stone. Four days later, in the CB Fisher Plate, Pike was on the outstanding English import Gothic but was convinced his mount couldn't stay the mile-and-a-half of the race. So he put £1000 on Statesman, and then went out and nursed Gothic to a clear victory.

Balloon King and Veilmond apart, the 1930 Derby was very ordinary. Of the 648 original entries for the race, only seven had made it to the start, and five of them were either out of form or not very good. The Doctor's Orders had promised much as a two-year-old but disappointed his trainer Jim Scobie with a shocking run in the Moonee Valley Cup, while the filly Miss Arrow hardly seemed likely to become the sixth of her sex since Briseis (1876) to win the classic. Wapilly was still in the Melbourne Cup as well as the Derby, but based on his form no one quite knew why.

Not surprisingly then, betting on the race was stifled. In the days leading up to the meeting, many punters had enquired about the Veilmond–Phar Lap Victoria Derby–Melbourne Cup double, and it was at a ridiculously short quote by the time the three-year-olds jumped away. Unfortunately, Sam Sullivan had come up with this double as his best chance of redemption and he plunged what little money he had on it, even though he knew deep down that the odds of 5–2 he was taking were ridiculously short. And within two furlongs of the start, he knew he was in trouble. The Doctor's Orders jumped to the lead, and Pike on Balloon King loped right in behind him, while back third,

Maurice McCarten on Veilmond was fighting with his mount, which seemed keen to get in towards the rail, rather than hold its place one off the fence. Miss Arrow was fourth, and the other three were already stragglers.

The Doctor's Orders led by as much as six lengths down by the abattoirs at the back of the course, around the six furlongs pole, but on the turn Pike made his move and the pacemaker quickly chucked it in. Veilmond and Miss Arrow emerged to challenge, but the odds-on favourite continued to duck in, hampering the filly while Balloon King booted clear. In the run to the line Pike was able to put the whip away and enjoy a one-and-a-half length victory. As horse and rider came back to the mounting yard, the consensus was that a more low-key Derby had never been run. Few thought Balloon King could get near Phar Lap in the Cup, a point Pike was happy to confirm when he spoke to reporters after the race, and it seemed that Veilmond was just not much good. Ned Moss wondered whether the problem might have been his jockey. McCarten might be a damn fine rider, one of the best to come over from New Zealand, but maybe he and Veilmond were like oil and water. They'd engaged the crack Sydney lightweight Billy Cook for the Cup, knowing that McCarten couldn't get down to 7.6, and that might prove a godsend. It was their only hope.

OVER ON THE OTHER side of Melbourne, at Beverley Street, Glenhuntly, Harry Telford was watching closely as Woodcock took Phar Lap off the float and back into Cripps' stables. He was even able to get into the kitchen to hear the Derby result on the wireless and was pleased that his trusted friend Pike had won again, and comforted, too, by Veilmond's poor showing — an emerging three-year-old had always been his biggest fear. Now it seemed that only Tregilla from that age group was any real concern. Gee, the cup of tea was actually tasting all right, but then Brophy entered the room and reality resurfaced. Telford knew that the detective didn't like the St Albans plan but as far as he was concerned that was Brophy's problem; the detective wasn't the one getting the threatening phone calls. What needed to be decided now were things like what time do we leave, who goes and who stays, who can be trusted and who can't. For the next few hours, at least until Mr Raymond came around at 6.30, Telford was going to stay put, Woodcock was going to be with the horse like he always was, they'd move Phar Lap from stall to stall every couple of hours or so, the police guard would remain in place, the kelpie's muzzle would stay on until sunset and Brophy could finally check out the corner of James and Etna Streets, maybe via Malvolio Street.

Unfortunately, Creed wasn't home. He had gone to the races after all, or so his wife said. Not to worry, Etna Street was just a few more yards up James Street, running west while Malvolio went east. Standing on the corner, Brophy could look up and see a tram running along Glenhuntly Road and just beyond that the now famous picture theatre where the Studebaker had parked. This was really the first chance he'd had to stop and think about things. He imagined Woodcock on the pony leading Phar Lap down towards him, and then turning into Etna Street in a panic and trying to open the back gate of the house on the corner. Then the car came flying around the corner, horn blaring, a double-barrelled shotgun pointing out the window ...

Horn blaring? What was the reason for that? To scare the horse or wake the neighbours? Already, Brophy was getting more than a little weary of the suggestion that the gunmen were just trying to scare Phar Lap, so he would bolt and injure himself. The whole idea that ruthless underworld figures facing financial ruin would come up with such a clumsy scheme seemed pretty bloody stupid to him. These people could be callous bastards. If they really wanted to shoot the horse, they would hardly have missed from 20 yards. People at the course he'd been talking to had likened it all to a scene out of a gangster movie, and the more he thought about it the more he realised they were dead right. Why not just shoot the horse and be done with it? When Squizzy Taylor wanted to get square with the people at Caulfield after they kicked him off the course as an 'undesirable' during the Caulfield Cup carnival of 1922, he burnt the Members Stand down. If Squizzy had wanted to stop Phar Lap, he would have stopped him. Not scared him.

Then there was the double-barrelled shotgun. By almost all accounts, only one shot was fired, even though it wouldn't have been any trouble at all for the gunman to fire twice. Given that he missed his target completely, it was hard to imagine it was overconfidence that stopped him pulling the second trigger. What was going on?

Brophy walked over to the fence, to locate the pellet marks that Saker had been unable to find earlier in the day. At least that's what he planned to do. But try as he might, and he scoured the entire fence along all its length from top to bottom, he couldn't find any pellets. In the fence, the hedge behind the fence, on the grass, the footpath, the road, nothing. This was getting ridiculous. If someone fires a cartridge of shotgun pellets at a fence 20 yards away there should be any number of pellets in the timber, spread over a circle at least half-a-yard wide. A heavy enough shot would have ripped a hole through the fence. If they'd fired at the ground in front of Woodcock, there'd be pellets in the pickets and plenty of others spread over a fairly wide area. They certainly wouldn't be impossible to find. What did Saker say? Some bloke had found a cardboard wad. Brophy was no ballistics expert but he knew that a blank charge could be made by packing a used cartridge case with gunpowder and a second-hand cardboard wad. The flash Studebaker, faces hidden by newspapers, horn blaring ...

What would genuine, hard-nosed, murderous thugs make of all this?

They'd probably be as confused as he was. Maybe the people who'd been threatening Telford had nothing to do with the shooting. If that was right, spiriting the horse off to a secret location mightn't be a bad idea — in fact, it'd probably be the best way to foil some dastardly plans still waiting to be hatched. But jeez, they were asking a lot of Phar Lap, taking him away in the middle of the night to some place he'd never seen before, then bringing him back just before the jump. Don't horses like routine?

Right at this moment, the detective had two things on his mind. One, he had to get back to the CIB's Russell Street headquarters to help Saker compose an account of the day's proceedings, though he wasn't exactly sure what should be put down on paper and what, at this point at least, should be left unreported. And two, he couldn't help thinking what a good bet Tregilla was in the Cup. The second favourite would be resting back in his stall while Phar Lap was being hauled all over the countryside. What Brophy had to do was get himself somewhere where there was a wireless so he could listen to the Hotham Handicap. Unless something ran an outstanding Cup trial in that race then he needed to get in touch with his bookie and hope he could still get the 5–1 about the three-year-old that had been on offer in some quarters back at the track.

CHAPTER EIGHT

NO SUCH THING AS
A CERTAINTY

AFTER SOULTON COULD DO no better than seventh at 20–1 in the Cantala Stakes, the Melbourne Cup watchers were left to hope that a genuine challenger to Phar Lap would emerge through the Hotham Handicap, but unfortunately runners not engaged in the Cup finished one, two, three in the last race on the Derby Day program. It completed a dreadful meeting for punters, with Phar Lap at prohibitive odds-on the only favourite to win on the day. Temptation led the Hotham field from the start, but was headed before the turn and beat only one horse home. John Buchan started favourite in the race and made a positive dash up towards the lead at the six furlongs, but he was struggling 200 yards from home. Muratti ran on fairly for fourth, suggesting he might be running into a little form, with First Acre on his tail, but Second Wind was terrible, third last after getting the run of the race. Some Quality was near the rear for most of the way, before passing a few stragglers in the straight. Though some punters tried to find positives, in reality it was impossible to imagine any of this lot getting near Phar Lap on the Tuesday; bookmakers predicted it would be at least 12–1 bar two when the Cup field jumped away.

At Russell Street, Brophy waited patiently for his bookie to ring him back and found in Harold Saker a firm believer in his theory that the shooting had been a stunt. However, even if they were right, it took little of the pressure off them. This was not just because grim threats were still about, but also because such was the turmoil around Phar Lap that whatever the circumstances of the shooting there would still be a clamour in the papers to arrest the culprits. So Saker's report played a straight bat:

Victoria Police

Criminal Offence Report
C.I. Branch, Melbourne District

Offence: Shooting with intent to maim an animal

Committed at: Near corner of James and Etna Streets, Glenhuntly

Date and hour: 6 a.m., 1st November 1930

On whom: H.R. Telford

Occupation and address: C/o Cripps' Stables, Beverley St., Glenhuntly

Date and hour reported to Police: 8 a.m. today

By whom reported: H.R. Telford

Name of persons offending or suspected, and if the latter, grounds of suspicion: Two men, names unknown

Description, and if identifiable: 1st. A man about 30 years, clean shaven, dark complexion, thin build; 2nd. Can only be described as a young looking man wearing a motor driver's peaked cap.

Direction supposed to be taken by offenders: Drove along Etna Street to Augusta Street, and then drove in the direction of Glenhuntly Road.

Steps taken, where information sent to, general remarks, &c.: While Trevor Woodcock, foreman employed by H. R. Telford, was leading the racehorse, Phar Lap, from the racecourse to the stables, at 6 a.m. this morning, two men, who were in a Studebaker motor car which bore the number 1556 on the front, fired a shot at the hind-quarters of Phar Lap which missed its mark. The car was a blue sedan. A reward of £100 has been offered by Mr. Davis for the arrest and conviction of the offenders.

Signed: H. Saker, Detective, 1/11/30

That would do for know. They'd get Senior Constable Davis to pen a more detailed analysis in the morning. By then they'd have the info on the rego numbers provided by Woodcock and Creed. One thing they were grateful for was the fact that there was no major Melbourne Sunday paper; the only journo who'd rung them in the last hour had been that bloke seeking more information for the Sydney *Truth*. His would be an interesting story — maybe they should ring Sydney in the morning and get someone to read it to them. Already, the latest Phar Lap reports on the wireless were featuring suggestions that the police had not been able to find, to quote one newsreader, 'any marks which might have been caused by bullets or shotgun pellets'.

'Jack, I tried to find someone at the course who could tell me who was behind it,' Saker said. 'Everyone wants to guess, but no one seems to know. But as one bloke said to me, whoever did it went to a hell of a lot of trouble for not much result.'

'What we really need is someone with a bit of evil in them,' Brophy replied. 'What's a good crime story without a villain?'

Saker laughed. He knew that if Brophy needed to find a crook to fit the mould, he could do it. 'There's actually a fair bit of admiration around the bookmakers for what the Phar Lap people are supposed to have done with the double, you know,' Saker said, in a voice that suggested he was more than a little impressed himself. 'And some people are carrying on as if no one's ever tried to make any money betting on the race. Seven years ago, Jim Scobie won the Cup first up with Bitalli and made a fortune. No one tried to shoot him.'

'That was the year of the strike,' Brophy jumped in, recalling the infamous police strike of 1923. He vividly remembered the anarchy, how ruffians took over the city streets in a Saturday night of rioting and looting, how trams were derailed, shop windows smashed, an ex-soldier murdered. That was Derby Day. By then, Bitalli had been backed in from 100–1 to 4–1 favourite, and the bookmakers were facing payouts of more than £200,000. 'If they'd had wanted to get up close to shoot him,' he snarled, 'there would have been constables waving them through.'

Back then, the rank and file had been complaining they were the lowest paid and worst treated policemen in the country. Matters had reached boiling point when a 'spook' system — senior constables, in plain clothes, monitoring how uniformed men patrolled their beats — was introduced, and after two constables were fined for having a cup of tea on duty, hundreds of officers walked off the job. As far as Jack Brophy was concerned, the Police Association lost him that day. Coppers don't strike. How lucky was it that the Army came to the rescue? A squad of special volunteers, most of them ex-AIF and led by Sir John

Monash, had been drafted by the government. Within two years, General Blamey was Commissioner.

'The other thing about Telford is that while everyone in racing sees him as a surly old bloke, they also regard him as straight up and down,' Saker turned the conversation back to the task at hand. The last thing he wanted to hear was Brophy going on about the police union again. 'I had two different bookies point out that as far as they know, Telford's never gone slow on Phar Lap.'

'What about last year?' Brophy responded. 'I thought they stopped him in the Cup.'

'Pike couldn't ride Phar Lap in the Cup last year,' Saker replied. 'Because he was a three-year-old, the horse only carried 7.6. Bobbie Lewis rode him, and the horse pulled him out of the saddle all the way. It was like they went 15 rounds for two miles. Lewis is a great jockey; he's won four Melbourne Cups and no other has done that, but he's also a mate of Eric Connolly, the big punter, who made a lot of money on Nightmarch, and a few people thought he might have been doing Connolly's dirty work. But most experts just think Telford put the wrong jockey on. Lewis didn't know the horse. You saw how Pike rode him today, let him bowl along, let Phar Lap run his own race. That's how they ride him. With most horses, that sort of tactic would kill them over two miles, but Phar Lap's a freak. He just keeps running.'

Saker loved talking about racing, and for the moment Brophy was perfectly content to listen, given they had no leads and he wasn't required back at Beverley Street until 7.30.

'Do you know that in Sydney last autumn he was in a race over two-and-a-quarter miles?' Saker continued. 'Billy Elliott was riding him, and the horse took off. Elliott couldn't hold him. Phar Lap broke all sorts of records, even though he walked the last furlong, when the jockey finally got a grip of him. He ran the first seven furlongs of that race faster than the Randwick seven-furlongs record, in a two-and-a-quarter miles race! Afterwards the stewards called in Roy Reed, the jockey of Nightmarch, which ran second, and accused him of going slow, but Reed pointed out that he'd also broken the track record, even though he got beat by a furlong. That was the end of that inquiry!

'The one bloke who might be a risk is Pike. I've never heard anything really bad about him, except that he likes a bet. It wouldn't surprise me if the bookmakers gave him a call.'

WHICH, THAT VERY NIGHT, is exactly what happened. Mick Polson, a trainer, punter — and a mate — was the intermediary, visiting Pike's hotel to pass on details of an inducement of £10,000 if the jockey went slow on the the favourite. 'Tell 'em what to do with the money,' was Pike's angry reaction. 'All I want to do is win the Cup.'

'I knew that's what you'd say,' Polson said. 'But I had to make the offer, mate. You know what they're like.'

And that was that. Soon after, Polson retreated, presumably to relay the bad news back to his contacts, and Pike was left to wonder if the locks on his hotel-room door and the nightwatchman downstairs were all the protection he'd be needing.

AT AROUND THE SAME time Pike and Polson were having their brief chat, Telford and Guy Raymond were sitting down for a cup of tea at Joe Cripps' place. Brophy arrived soon after; Saker got the rest of the night off, after it was agreed that he needed to be at Caulfield racecourse by six the following morning. The two detectives had discussed whether they should let Telford and Raymond in on their prank theory, but as it was only speculation they thought it best to let things lie. For all the detectives' cynicism towards the 'shooting', they had to keep remembering there was still plenty of bad feeling out there towards Telford and quite a few bookmakers and punters who'd lose a lot of money if the favourite won the Cup. It'd be just Brophy's luck to announce it was all a joke and then something go horribly wrong.

So Telford and Raymond were free to go ahead with their mission. They'd wait until the early hours of Sunday morning, let's say 2am. They'd get Stan Boyden to back the float up as close as he could to the front gate, and put straw, mats and sugar bags down on the concrete to soften the scuff of the hooves as the horse walked from his stall. At this point, Boyden knew he was required, but had no idea where he was going. Who else needed to know? Woodcock would travel in the float with a constable, and another policeman would follow on a motor bike. Cripps needed to know that the champ was leaving, but his staff could work it out for themselves. They'd rouse Bobby Parker, who was boarding with another of Telford's apprentices, Jack Martin, above a shop up on Glenhuntly Road, just before it was time to go to Geelong. Pike was best left in the dark — that way, if someone asked him where his Cup mount was, he could honestly declare that he didn't know. Telford would drive down behind them in a separate car, but then return immediately and stay in Melbourne. He knew that from the moment the press cottoned on to the fact that Phar Lap was missing, the story would spread like a scrubfire, and it was better he was here to not talk to reporters rather than have them out all over the place looking for him. David Davis? 'I'll tell him in the morning,' Telford growled, 'when it's too late for him to change my mind.'

What about the police at Geelong? 'A good mate of mine is in charge down there,' Brophy said. 'I'll let him know what's going on, but I doubt there's any reason to tell anyone else. You've got two of my men travelling with you — they can stay until you're settled, and I'll send as many as you need on Tuesday, to escort Phar Lap back to Flemington.'

And, really, that was it. Short of the gangsters staking out the stable and then following the float on the open highway, this was as good a strategy as any. Indeed, as they went through the list of people who'd know about what was going on from start to finish — Telford, Raymond, Brophy, Saker, Woodcock, Parker, Boyden, Davis in the morning, two constables and a Police Commissioner — the plan started to seem almost foolproof. So Brophy and Raymond were on their way, Cripps came in and suggested he and Telford share a bottle of Foster's, and, after a briefing, Woodcock went back to check again on his horse.

NO ONE WAS HAPPIER about the St Albans plan than Tommy Woodcock, who by now was a nervous wreck. What he really wanted to do was have a kip, but there was no chance — the slightest noise and he was wide awake, and in a stable with horses rustling about there were plenty of slightest noises. One comment from the track kept reverberating in his head: 'Jeez, Tommy,' said a mate in the mounting yard, 'shouldn't they be conducting an attempted murder investigation?'

He was lucky to be alive and totally unprepared for all that was happening to him. He'd been born 25 years ago, in a little place called Uralgurra, near Kempsey on the NSW north coast. In 1911, his father took his Cobb & Co. coach business 60 miles south, to Port Macquarie, which is where Tommy fell for horses, under the tutelage of a knockabout named Billy Fuller. It was Mr Fuller who taught him how to ride, and the art of 'strapping'.

'A boy was called a "strapper" because when you cleaned and dressed a horse properly, you had a nice flat towel and you used to hit them on all the muscles,' Woodcock once said, remembering his days with Mr Fuller. 'You went from his neck right down his shoulders and along his back and along his rump and all down. The strapping noise was the noise of the towel hitting the muscles, to bring the muscles up and relax them.

'You think it was easy, but strapping was, properly done like that, a fairly strenuous sort of work. It brings the muscles up on you as well as the horse.'

Actually, a strapper did a lot more than that with his horses, but that was where the term came from. You needed to love horses to be good at it. When Tommy was 12, Mr Fuller suggested he head to Sydney to try his luck as a jockey. No doubt the fact that the lad much preferred stables to schoolyards would have motivated this advice. So Tommy jumped on the train with his mother, and landed at the Randwick stables of Dick O'Connor, who'd trained Piastre to win the Melbourne Cup in 1912. First night, the bell went for dinner and the novice was left at the post — by the time Tommy got to the table even his bread and butter were gone. 'You'll 'ave to smarten your footwork up, son, if you want to eat round 'ere,' one of the experienced lads quipped. Then Tommy found that his bed was dirty, so he half-slept in a chair all night and in the morning went to find Mum, who was staying two or three miles away in Redfern, to tell her they were going home. But Mrs Woodcock found her son a second chance, with another Randwick trainer, Barney Quinn, and that worked out much better. Mr Quinn polished the diamond Mr Fuller had cut. 'You'll never learn on quiet horses,' Mr Quinn would say. 'You've got to learn on something that'll do something wrong.'

When Tommy had his first race ride he was 5 stone 4, but by 1927 he'd 'ballooned' out to 8.4 and had to give the race-riding game away. He took a variety of jobs, including working on building sites, but what he wanted to do was stay with the horses, so if he could ever pinch some work as a track rider or a strapper with one of the smaller stables he did so. One of the trainers he did some work for was Harry Telford.

Telford was a native of Ballarat, in country Victoria, where his father was something of a racing man, helping train horses owned by the town's leading publican, Mr Walter Craig. Among these was Nimblefoot, a handy stayer that won fame for his owner in somewhat macabre circumstances in 1870. In February of that year, Mr Craig sought odds about a Metropolitan Handicap–Melbourne Cup double involving a moderately performed horse named Croydon and his own Nimblefoot, and the prominent bookmaker Joe Slack offered £1000 to a round of drinks, which the publican quickly accepted, not least because the men were drinking in his hotel. A few months later, Craig dreamt every owner's fantasy — Nimblefoot, wearing his distinctive violet colours, won the Cup — but the vision had an eerie sidelight, for the jockey was a wearing a black armband. Therefore, he sadly told his friends the next morning, if his dream was true he'd not be at Flemington to see his horse triumph. Walter Craig was only 45, but later that very day he died.

Croydon duly won the 'Metrop', and then Nimblefoot entered Cup calculations with a sudden return to form in the Hotham Handicap. The *Age* reported the whole astonishing story 24 hours *before* the Cup, and the following day, with jockey Johnny Day wearing a crepe black armband, Nimblefoot prevailed narrowly over Lapdog in a tight finish. On the following Monday, Joe Slack was at the Goydor Hotel in the city, nobly counting out 20 fifties to a gentleman from Ballarat, a friend of Mrs Craig.

Years later, Harry Telford left his father and went to New Zealand, where for a period he was the foreman for Richard

Mason, who found his greatest fame as the trainer of Gloaming. By this time, though, Telford was back in Australia, training with little success at Newcastle, north of Sydney, and then at Randwick. His best horse was the stayer Ard-na-ree, which was good enough to run in the 1918 Melbourne Cup. However, there was precious little else.

Through the 1920s, Telford was consistently unlucky. When Phar Lap won his first race, a mediocre two-year-old handicap at Rosehill in Sydney in April 1929, the narrow victory, after the gelding was backed from 15–1 into sevens, gave Telford the chance to pay his debts and have enough left over to offer some more work to Woodcock in the following spring. It was then that the affinity between horse and strapper blossomed, so when Telford needed someone to take his new star south for the Victoria Derby and the Melbourne Cup, he asked Woodcock to become his full-time stable foreman, first task to go to Melbourne. Tommy, totally enamoured of his mate, couldn't accept the offer quick enough.

'Stable foreman' sounded important, but while Telford was certainly on the up after Phar Lap's success in the Rosehill Guineas and the AJC Derby, his was still a small-scale operation. Woodcock was really still a strapper, just now a full-time one rather than sharing the load with others, which meant he had to be up and about at four in the morning every day, wet or dry, to take the horses out of their stalls. He'd muck out their stables, get them ready for trackwork, take them to trackwork, bring them home. Then he'd groom them — using a softer brush for the coat; a harder one, more like a broom, for the mane and tail, and to get the mud off their legs. A smart strapper could tell by the shine in a horse's coat if the animal was fit and healthy. Every afternoon or early evening, Woodcock would clean and grease his horses' feet with lanolin, wash their eyes and nostrils, then lift their tails and clean their backsides. At night, a horse had to be nice and comfortable, with just the right amount of hay and fresh water in his stall. With Bobby, Woodcock sometimes took to sleeping in the stall or on a mattress nearby, as if that was the only way he could convince himself his mate was truly comfortable.

The pay was low, which meant he couldn't bet much, even if he'd wanted to. But being so close to the sport's heartbeat, he knew there was no such thing as a certainty, so that was no great sacrifice. Around the track, his fellow workers were a crew so motley that he'd toughened up real quick (though he never lost the angelic looks that made middle-aged women want to mother him). For every heart of gold, there was a rat's cunning and strappers got none of the champagne the members drink on race day. But there was the joy of working with horses and the satisfaction that came with seeing a galloper in your care turn into a good one.

That was always the key. People try to be romantic, but racing is about one thing: winning. Every early morning, every gallop, every oat, every strand of hay, every strap of the towel, every night's sleep was done to get a horse ready to race. If a horse can't win, move on to the next one. Don't waste time; get too close to a horse at your peril. Up at four, in bed by eight, asleep by a minute past. The involvement was total, and had to be. For a strapper, racing is the most important thing there is. Actually, it's the only thing. Tommy knew all this, so while he'd never admit it, there was no doubt that Phar Lap's unique ability played a part in the extraordinary bond that formed between them. When he took his horse to the races and proudly led him around the mounting yard, and then quietly watched as Pike guided the champ to victory after victory — that was the ultimate job satisfaction.

Still, there was no doubt either that the bond he and Bobby had was as tight as any strapper–racehorse relationship. Jim Pike would tell the story of taking the champion out on to the training track at Randwick one morning, and quickly feeling that something wasn't right. Phar Lap wouldn't put any effort into his work, and Pike slowed him down, fearing an injury. However, there was nothing amiss. Finally, they cantered him around a corner and there was Tommy in the distance. Bobby wanted to be taken over to his friend, for a freshly plucked piece of grass and to have his nose rubbed, before going to work.

Being Phar Lap's strapper should have been the best job in the world, but right now it wasn't. Dodging bullets had never been in the job description. Instead of being as fast asleep as his weariness said he should be, he was in the middle of one of those off again, on again naps where it's not until you're woken with a start that you realise you've been asleep at all. It wasn't Telford knocking on the stable door that woke him or Phar Lap fidgeting nearby — it was that damned guard dog growling in his sleep. It was 12.20am. Tommy tried again, but then the wind in the trees woke him, or was it footsteps? Half twelve. An hour later, when the boss finally came, Woodcock was impatient, ready to go. The float driver would be here in 15 minutes.

Stan Boyden duly arrived, and the first thing he said was, 'Where are we going, Tommy?'

To which Woodcock replied, 'I'll tell you in a minute. Did you see anyone on the street?'

Boyden shook his head. Telford finished checking the bags on the concrete, a constable returned to say that the coast was clear, Woodcock roused the horse and then they got him onto the float as quietly as possible. More quickly than they could have imagined, they were on their way, with Telford following in his car at a safe distance. The old trainer tried to concentrate on keeping Boyden's old Brockway float in view, but more often than not he found himself either checking to see if they were being followed or, even worse, thinking rather mournfully about all that had happened in the past 21 hours. His father had taught him, and his own life in racing had shown him how finely tuned racehorses hate being unsettled. Phar Lap had been shot at, surrounded by strangers to and fro' the races and at the track itself, won a top-class race in near record time and then, at two o'clock in the bloody morning, been woken up and sent off on a journey to a place he'd never seen. What sort of mug trainer would do that to his horse?

Throughout what proved to be an uneventful journey to Geelong and then all the way back to Cripps' stable, Telford couldn't help but think that it was not only his champion who was leaving him — so, too, was his dream of winning the Melbourne Cup.

CHAPTER NINE

PHAR LAP HYSTERIA

IN NORMAL CIRCUMSTANCES, WITH Phar Lap having come through the Melbourne Stakes so well, Harry Telford would have been tempted to take him down to Caulfield on Sunday, just for a canter and a look around. After all, the big chestnut had been to Caulfield at dawn every morning in the lead-up to Derby Day. Instead, he stayed right away from the place. All his horses stayed at home, he was as fidgety and crotchety as he'd ever been, but at least he knew Phar Lap was safely ensconced at St Albans, and he was also reasonably confident that for the moment at least there wasn't a gangster or pressman in Melbourne who was aware of that. Guy Raymond had called at 7am, as had been arranged, to make sure Telford got back to the city in one piece, to say that it seemed the horse had handled the trip better than could be expected, and that Woodcock was refusing all invitations to get some sleep.

Those who did venture to Caulfield were on the lookout for gangster types and suspicious-looking vehicles every step of the way. Officially, the track was shut on Sundays, but the trainers were still able to give their horses exercise, and in Cup week that meant the track watchers, some reporters and a few of the keener form students were there in case anything happened. Inevitably, all eyes were out for Phar Lap, even though some pessimists had resolved to stay as far away from the horse as possible if he did venture to the track. There was always the chance that a sniper was lurking beyond the outside rail of the course proper or maybe up near those trees at the seven furlongs start, so why take any chances? Detective Saker simply hung around the infield of the track, near where the trainers usually congregated to give instructions to jockeys and watch their prized possessions go about their exercise.

Only rarely would an owner enter this closeted little world, but this morning Saker noticed Bill Sewell, racing writer from the Adelaide *Register*, talking to Harry Lewis, the well-known South Australian racing identity. Mr Lewis' mare Nadean, given an outside hope in the Melbourne Cup by some observers, was going once around the steeplechase track. Lewis had come down from the grandstand to talk to his trainer, Bill Brodie, and, as he freely admitted, to get the latest word on Phar Lap, when the reporter caught up with him.

The sight of an owner up at 6am on a Sunday to watch his horse canter slowly around the track made Saker stop and ponder just how totally the racing game could entrap some people. He also looked at Mr Lewis and said very quietly to himself, 'There's another person who'd benefit from Phar Lap not running.' With the favourite in the field, Nadean would be 25–1 or longer. Take him out, or make the job impossible for him, and suddenly Harry Lewis was the owner of a 10–1 chance. Saker thought of other prominent owners with horses in the Cup field, distinguished men such as Mr Mackinnon and Mr Lee Steere, who dreamt of winning the Cup. John Wren, too. They all had a motive. Quickly, though, Saker shook off those suspicions about the Establishment, and instead went searching for anyone who knew something he didn't.

However, he soon discovered that a wall of silence was now firmly in place. Whether each trainer had decided off his own bat that no one was going to say anything to anyone or whether the word had been passed around, Saker wasn't sure, but judging by the way the stablehands, strappers and track riders shook their heads and said they knew nothing, it seemed now that Manchester Grove had actually been totally deserted except for Woodcock, Phar Lap and the Studebaker. Saker sensed that the lack of co-operation wasn't due to any particular antipathy towards the police; it was more a fear that the thugs behind the shooting might target the person who said the wrong thing. It was better to be safe than very sorry. He did learn that over at Flemington George Price had put an armed guard outside Veilmond's stall, apparently in response to some crank calls he'd received before the Derby. Until the Phar Lap shooting, Price had figured his usual security — trusted staff, a strong lock and an angry blue cattle dog — would be enough. Not any more.

As the sun introduced more light into the early morning, Saker wonderedwhere else this fear might spread. Meanwhile, as far as the Phar Lap shooting was concerned all he and Brophy had was a reasonable picture of the car and lousy descriptions of the men inside, two different number plates whose owner or owners, most likely, had no possible link to the Studebaker, plenty of motive, no one talking, no pellets on the street or in the fence, and one cardboard wad. And no one from the stables talking. That left the blokes from the papers.

The track watchers (or 'track representatives' as the papers liked to more grandly call them) — one each from the *Argus* and the *Age* and one, James Creed, who acted for the *Herald*, the *Sun News-Pictorial* and the *Sporting Globe* — had as usual been joined by enthusiasts working for specialist weekly racing papers such as the *Sporting Judge*. These men came to the course every morning, rain or shine, cold or chilly, stopwatches in hand, to time the gallops, glean some inside info, unmask 'smokies' being set for a coup. This latter information might help them make a living, otherwise track watching was a second job that paid miserable wages but gave them a part in the racing game. Creed was a little fellow in his early fifties, his face partly hidden by a cloth cap pulled tight over his eyebrows, his manner gruff. He worked as a clerk during the day after keeping a close eye on the horses before breakfast.

'No, I've got nothing to add to what I said to the policeman yesterday,' was his curt reply after Saker asked, 'Would one of you gentlemen be James Creed?'

'I see,' Saker responded quietly. 'Why then did you say so much more to the *Herald* on Saturday than you said to us?'

'I don't know whether I did. They might have just made more of it. I do work for them, you know.'

Saker cut straight to the chase — the inconsistency between Creed's memory and the evidence provided to Senior Constable Davis by Leonard Searle. When exactly did Creed see that blue, maybe green Studebaker?

'Must've been round five, maybe a bit after.'

'The blokes in the car, can you tell me what they looked like?'

Of course, he couldn't, really. 'Like I said yesterday, they had newspapers over their faces, so I couldn't get a look at them. Didn't want to look at them either. One was fat. They were young blokes, really. Sorry, I can't help you more than that.'

'And it was definitely around five?'

'Could've been later, I suppose. You see I was running late, I'm usually here by five. It wouldn't have looked good if I'd missed Phar Lap ...'

'If you were going to sleep in, Jim,' a younger fellow butted in, 'today was the morning to do it, not yesterday.'

Everyone in the small group laughed, including Saker. He always enjoyed being among racing people. They were usually street smart, always had a hardness about them, but a genuineness, too. 'And who might you be, mate?' he turned to the bloke who'd interrupted.

'Bill Hall is my name, from the *Argus*, sir,' the man replied. 'I'm here every morning with Jim.'

'What do you make of Phar Lap not being here?' Saker asked as he looked Hall over. Hall was a little bloke in his early thirties, if that, clad in a dark grey vest and jacket that contrasted quite starkly with Creed's old brown cardigan.

'Dunno. It'd be a bit strange them taking him somewhere else to exercise, when he's only stabled down the road.'

Hall was more outgoing than Creed, a man who stood out rather than blended into his surroundings. Saker learnt that he'd been a jockey, but the weight had beaten him, so now he had ambitions of becoming a journalist. Watching the gallops at Caulfield for one of the city's main papers was a start.

'Those blokes over there,' Hall continued, pointing at the reporters, 'have heard a whisper he might be hurt. They were hoping Telford might be here, but even if he was I doubt the cranky bastard would have told them anything. Strewth, he's making life hard for them. And Bradman arrives in Melbourne this afternoon. They're worried cricket's going to get the front page tomorrow. In Cup week!'

Hall was referring to the fact that the Australian cricket team, fresh from a victorious tour of England, was in the middle of a triumphant city-by-city return home. They'd landed in Perth earlier in the week, and now most of the team were in Adelaide. Don Bradman, whose unprecedented batting feats during the tour had captivated the nation, was travelling ahead of the rest of the squad, and was due to land at Essendon Airport, just north of Melbourne, that afternoon.

'And what about the shooting? What have you heard?'

'It's all part of the Phar Lap hysteria,' Hall spoke very seriously, like a radio newsreader announcing a major story about the King.

'What? So you don't think it's real?' Saker *was* very serious.

'Aw, no, it's real. I mean, it's like it was inevitable,' Hall's tone changed. Suddenly, it was as if he was being interrogated. The copper had conned him with all that 'matey' talk. 'Ever since Amounis won here, Phar Lap was going to be shot, bombed, doped or something,' he went on, trying too hard not to trip over his tongue.

'Detective,' a real reporter butted in, 'the word is you didn't find any pellets at the scene. I believe the *Truth* in Sydney is running that line. Is that rumour true?'

'I'm not going to comment on rumours,' Saker responded.

'Any news on the car?'

'We should have information on the plate numbers some time today.'

'Are you close to an arrest?'

'Not at this moment, gentlemen.' Now Saker was being interrogated! He hadn't come here to give a press conference, and having spoken to Creed he felt he had all he was likely to get. 'As soon as we have anything for you, either I or more likely Detective-Sergeant Brophy will let you know. Good day to you all.'

THE TRUTH IN SYDNEY had gone with the 'they were only trying to scare the horse' angle. First thing after he arrived at the station, Jack Brophy had organised for the front-page story to be read to a stenographer, so that when Saker arrived it was there waiting for him to read. The report, headlined 'WILL GUN SHOT FRIGHTEN PHAR LAP INTO CUP WIN?', began breathlessly:

> The affair is without parallel in the history of horse racing in Australia; it reads like a chapter from a Nat Gould novel. The only thing missing is that there isn't a trainer, a jockey or an owner whose winning of the hand and heart of some beautiful maiden depends upon Phar Lap's success in the Cup.
>
> It would have been wonderful if things could have been arranged that way. But it looks as though the crooks who indulge in horse maiming or doping have no soul for romance ...

For the first two-thirds, the story focused on the dastardly nature of the attack, quoting liberally from Senior Constable Davis' notes, sometimes taking things to extremes. The line about the car trying to run Woodcock over was a new one. They also had the make of the car wrong (apparently it was now a 'new bluish-coloured Minerva'), they reckoned Phar Lap was stabled with Joe Bird, they said the investigation 'had been placed in the hands of Detective Harold Saker', and at the conclusion of the article they tipped Tregilla to win the Cup. 'One out of four ain't bad,' said Brophy. Halfway down the fifth column, this was thrown into the mix:

> The failure of the police investigating the Phar Lap affair to find any pellets lends color to the theory that the gun might have held a blank and that the miscreant's intention was not to

wound or kill the horse, but to frighten him in the hope that he would break away and injure himself sufficiently to prevent him running in the Cup.

A search was made today for pellets, but not even a mark of one was found ...

Adding weight to this aspect of the story was Sydney racing's chief stipendiary steward, Mr McMahon, being quoted as having quite a chuckle when invited by *Truth* to discuss what the paper was now calling the 'alleged attempt to shoot Phar Lap in Melbourne'.

'The man with the gun must have been a terribly bad shot,' McMahon chortled.

Before Brophy and Saker could contemplate the chief stipe's sense of humour, a constable walked in with information on the number plates. Woodcock's plate had last been registered to a Mr George Baxter, who until recently had worked as a mine manager at Walwa in southern NSW, 45 miles from Albury. Yet the contact addresses they'd come up with for Baxter were c/- the White Tank Hotel at West Wyalong, 120 miles north of the NSW–Victoria border, and a residence in Davis Street, South Yarra, one of Melbourne's finer suburbs. The sergeant at Wodonga, the town across the Murray River from Albury, thought Baxter might have moved to Adelaide. 'This is all very helpful,' Brophy muttered. Motor registry records stated that Baxter's car was an old model yellow Paige, and that the registration had been cancelled in April.

Creed's plate number had last been registered to an Edward Trudgett, but was cancelled five years ago. 'I wonder if that's the footballer Ted Trudgett,' Saker said. 'He's playing up in the bush now.'

'If the rego's been dead for five years or more,' Brophy replied. 'I don't think we need to pursue that one either.'

What angle should they pursue? The *Sun*, another Sunday paper from Sydney, had run a page-one story written by their Melbourne correspondent that predicted the gangsters' next move would be to bomb Phar Lap's stable. The fact was, Brophy sighed, they had bugger all to go on. He had hoped James Creed would provide a description of the men in the Studebaker, but he either couldn't or wouldn't help. If the racing world had shut up shop, as Saker said they had, he knew the underworld would be an even harder nut to crack, and he didn't really fancy a day using up valuable contacts on what could easily be a wild goose chase. Maybe the best bet was just to make sure Phar Lap was safe, confirm Pike was all right, get the Cup over and done with, and then move on to other things.

'Let's get back down to James and Etna,' he said, 'then go and see Telford again, to make sure he's happy with the security arrangements, then knock on a few doors to see if anyone knows something they shouldn't. If we do that, when General Blamey comes looking for an update on Monday, we should be able to accommodate him.'

IF THE DETECTIVES EXPECTED to have the crime scene to themselves they were disappointed. There might have been 50 people in the vicinity, as if it was a tourist attraction, reliving the car's swoop round the corner, mimicking the blast of the shotgun, pointing from the corner back at the picture theatre, saying how brave the 'lad riding Phar Lap' must have been. Brophy pulled his homburg hard over his forehead, but was still quickly recognised by a trio of reporters, one accompanied by a photographer, all anxious to update him.

'Detective, reports have stated that there were no pellets found at the scene,' one said excitedly. 'What then is your reaction to the discovery this morning of a number of pellets in the fence and on the ground?'

Brophy wanted to say, 'That's the first I've heard of it.' Actually, he wanted to say something a lot worse than that. Instead, he just grunted, while Saker asked, with a hint of embarrassment, to be shown exactly where these pellets might have been found. Guided to a place a few yards closer to James Street than he'd believed Woodcock and Phar Lap had been when the shot was fired, but still one he had inspected the previous afternoon, Brophy bent down to see a handful of pellets lying on the grass. At the same time, the reporters were eagerly pointing at what looked like shot marks on the picket fence.

'Do you know who found them?' the detective asked.

'No, I don't,' the reporters replied in unison.

The picket fence, four feet high, ran along the front of the property in James Street and around into Etna Street for about half the length of the house; at that point it joined the six-foot high paling fence that ran to the back of the property. Behind the picket fence was a cypress hedge. Back on Derby Day morning, Woodcock had tried to open the gate into the backyard, and then backed Phar Lap up against the palings when the Studebaker charged around the corner. A bit more than 24 hours later, the journalists were showing the detectives what appeared to be pellet marks on a large branch in the hedge. Closer to ground level, two pellets could be clearly seen embedded in one of the pickets, and Brophy was about to dig them out when the photographer stepped forward and asked if he could take a picture first. Which he did, with his reporter's index finger measuring the width between the first pellet and the second.

Wedged against the fence was a newspaper, and Brophy picked it up and to his astonishment found that it had pellet marks all through it. The newspaper lads had missed this, but now they quickly went for their notebooks and the detectives knew that the 'pellet-riddled' paper would be getting a prominent run in tomorrow's fish-and-chips wrappers. Brophy and Saker walked across the road, chatted for a couple of minutes, and then the senior detective called the reporters over.

'I'm sorry, gentlemen, but at this point I haven't really got much to say,' he began. 'Inquiries are proceeding slowly. This definite evidence suggests that the charge was fired from about three feet six inches off the ground and at an angle of 45 degrees. The object of the men was to wound Phar Lap in the flanks and so injure him that he would have to be withdrawn from the Melbourne Cup. That is all for the moment. Good day.'

On the way back to their car, Saker couldn't help but ask, 'Jack, what was all that stuff about the shot being fired from about three feet six inches off the ground? Where else could it have been shot from? It wasn't like they were standing on the roof when they fired the gun. And the "45 degrees" business? If they shot at an angle of 45 degrees they would've hit the road about three-and-a-half feet in front of them, not wounded Phar Lap's flanks.'

Brophy shuffled in his seat, and then slowly turned and looked at his partner. 'Harold, mate,' he said, 'I bet they'll quote me word for word.'

CHAPTER TEN

TUESDAY CAN'T COME QUICK ENOUGH

FOR ALMOST ALL THE players involved in the Phar Lap drama, the rest of Sunday went pretty much without incident. Unless you count the fact that every 15 minutes or so a member of the public contacted Russell Street to pass on the latest piece of gossip or to provide the critical tip-off that would save the horse from impending doom. Every man, woman and child in Melbourne was talking about 'Big Red'. Out at Essendon Airport, as more than 5000 people waited to see Don Bradman touch down, you could count on one hand the people who weren't offering their two bob's worth about the latest Cup news.

'If you owned Phar Lap, and you'd received death threats,' someone asked, 'would you still run him in the Cup?'

'Yeah, I would, definitely,' his mate replied.

'What if the gun was aimed at you, rather than the horse?'

Most people laughed, if a little uneasily. For some, the Cup and the fate of its favourite were matters far too serious for jokes.

Much funnier was a story about Bradman's train trip from Perth to Adelaide, which was doing the rounds after first being aired on the wireless earlier in the day. About 250 miles north of Adelaide, not too far from Port Augusta, is a little town called Woocalla, and word had got out that Bradman's train was coming through. So a big crowd turned up, hoping for a glimpse of the batsman who had scored one triple century, two double centuries and a century in the recent Ashes series in England, but it was three o'clock in the morning when the train stopped. Not surprisingly, the great one was fast asleep.

'What are you doing out at this hour?' the guard asked one well-dressed lad on the platform when the train ground to a halt.

'We want to see Don Bradman,' the boy promptly replied.

'Righto son, up on my shoulder,' said the guard, and he lifted the startled young fan up so his face was close to a first-class carriage. 'That's him, through the window, in his pyjamas.'

The child, inevitably, was awestruck at having seen his hero 'in the flesh'. What wouldn't the English bowlers have done to have caught Bradman napping!

THAT SCENE AT WOOCALLA station occurred around the same time Stan Boyden's trusty float was being greeted by Guy Raymond at St Albans. A few hours later, and you wouldn't have thought Phar Lap had missed a good night's sleep, but the same could not be said about Tommy Woodcock, who appeared to be in something of a trance as he walked his friend slowly around the paddocks. He was almost too tired to worry if anyone was spying through the tall hedges that surrounded the property, but when the engine of a truck on the road that ran past the property misfired just as he took Phar Lap onto the now disused old training track, poor Tommy's heart missed one hell of a beat. Mr Raymond's offer of a bed for the night would have to be rejected. The strapper would be sleeping with his horse.

BACK IN THE CITY, Brophy and Saker met David Davis at the Menzies Hotel, on the corner of Bourke and William Streets, where the American and his wife were staying, and found him pretty gung-ho about the need to catch the crooks but not as keen to talk about the wagers he had made that had reputedly upset the bookmakers so much. What the detectives couldn't work out was whether the American was all bluster when it came to the punt, or whether he really had a damn good hand that he wanted to keep close to his chest. More likely the former, they reckoned, a view that the interstate pressmen staying at the New Treasury Hotel in Spring Street seemed to confirm.

The consensus among the writers from Sydney was that when it came to the punt, Davis was hardly a major player. A group of big gamblers led by Eric Connolly had ingratiated themselves with Davis in the hope that such an alliance would give them inside information on Phar Lap, and maybe a say in the planning of his race schedule. However, they'd organised this without realising that Telford's crusty persona and testy relationship with Davis meant that it was unlikely to happen. Still, when Connolly and some big punters connected to the Amounis camp, most notably Maude Vandenburg, came up with the idea of the Cups double sting, Davis assured them he could get Telford onside. Which he did, but it had cost him a half-share in the horse when Telford's lease ran out in January. Davis, the reporters guessed, might have had the double running for two or three thousand quid. He'd probably outlaid 100 pound, 200 at the most. Mrs Vandenburg, they knew, had it going for twenty grand.

What Connolly's final profit would be was anyone's guess. The man was highly organised and very clever, using a network of agents from around the country to put his bets on in small doses with many different registered bookmakers and illegal SPs. This allowed him to avoid scrutiny and maximised his chances of obtaining top odds. Betting in this way also made it impossible for others to measure just how big the plunge was. Further clouding the picture, Connolly sold his tips for a living and in that game success breeds success, so it was in his interest to unashamedly promote his coups and his cunning. Brophy remembered Harry Telford saying that Connolly was a man who always talked up his winnings. The press seemed happy to play along with this charade, never questioning Connolly's accounting methods. Just last Wednesday, in the Sydney sporting paper, the *Referee*, he had claimed to have backed Tregilla in July or August at 200–1 to win the Melbourne Cup, and to have continued to back the colt for 'thousands more'. Of course, the paper paid tribute to Connolly's 'uncanny instinct for detecting horses likely to improve'. But was he really as clever as he seemed? It certainly was amazing how many 'leviathan' punters, men who were reported as betting — and making — tens of thousands of pounds every Saturday, ended up dying with hardly a zac to their name.

And bookmakers love to exaggerate their losses, as if they deserve our sympathy. At the New Treasury, the detectives learned that Connolly had told two Sydney reporters, Cliff Graves and Bert Wolfe — confidentially, of course, and in separate conversations so that both journos had the 'scoop' — that he had the double running for £200,000. In all probability that was more like the total figure the bookies would be paying out to punters all over the country, but it was Connolly's style to claim the lot for himself. Would 200,000 quid be the worst result ever for bookmakers? Graves and Wolfe doubted it. Certainly, the depression meant there were fewer 'little' punters risking a bet, and Phar Lap had been a short price from the opening markets, so there had been minimal opportunity for the bagmen to balance their ledgers, once the big bets went on. Thus, even if the total payout wasn't going to be a record, the losses might be heavier than usual. Brophy told the reporters that he knew of only one registered bookmaker in Melbourne who'd go under if Phar Lap won. The reporters thought there might be a couple at most in Sydney in a similar boat, but added that it was like that most years, especially lately. Bookmaking was a risky business. The fear was that there were unscrupulous, unlicensed bookies in trouble; they were the operators Telford had most reason to fear.

Saker wanted to chase up some contacts in Collingwood, but Brophy stayed to spend an enjoyable hour with Wolfe, as the racing writer for the *Daily Guardian*, *Daily Telegraph* and *Sunday Sun* shared stories of what had clearly been a colourful life. Too young to enlist at the start of the War, he had served in France from 1916 before returning home to a career in sports journalism that saw him become the racing editor for the *Referee* in 1923, when he was only 25. Two years later he moved to Melbourne, as sports editor for the *Argus* and the *Australasian*, but then he opted for a rather drastic career change, moving to Queensland to become a stipendiary steward. He stayed on that side of the racing industry for four years, and then returned to what he loved most, race writing, taking up his current position about 12 months back. Throughout his career, he'd written under the nom de plume of 'Cardigan', paying homage to Lord Cardigan, the horse owned by his grandfather, Mr John Mayo, that upset the great mare Wakeful in the Cup of 1903.

Wolfe told a terrific yarn from that famous day. All of six years young, it was his first Cup, and he was thrilled to be accompanying his beloved grandfather. Mr Mayo was quietly confident, but their journey to Flemington was interrupted by a funeral procession, and it was risking monstrous luck to cut across in front of the casket. Instead, they went a back way, where they ran into a prominent Melbourne bookmaker who was also on his way to the track. 'Confident?' asked the bookie. 'What price will you offer?' shot back Mayo, and quickly a bet of £12,000 to £2000, odds of 6–1, was negotiated. Challenged to take another £5000 to £1000, Mayo accepted, giving him a potential profit of £17,000. The bookmaker had no idea that the owner was so sure of victory that he'd already prepared a telegram to his wife back in Sydney, which read: 'The colt won.' Immediately after the race, he contacted the telegraph office as arranged, with simple, triumphant instructions: 'Send it.' The funeral had only been unlucky for some.

SAM SULLIVAN WAS BROPHY'S expert when it came to the history of Melbourne Cup plunges, so when the two got together around five o'clock, the bookmaker soon found himself retelling stories of successful and foiled betting stings from days gone by. Top of his list was 1877, when Mr Herbert Power's little grey colt Savanaka overcame enormous difficulties to almost pull off a coup that had been 12 months in the making. As a two-year-old, Savanaka had just two starts, both over six furlongs, for one win and was then taken back to St Albans Stud, where his trainer James Wilson kept him out of view until after the Melbourne Cup weights for 1877 were released. The result was that he was given the featherweight of 6.2, which precipitated a plunge worth more than £40,000 if it came true.

Meanwhile, in Sydney, a colt by the name of Chester, trained by Etienne de Mestre and owned by the breeder, pastoralist and parliamentarian, the Hon. James White, was also being heavily backed, to the point that in straight-out Cup betting and in markets on the Victoria Derby–Melbourne Cup double he was supported to win £80,000. De Mestre was something of a genius when it came to the Cup, most famous for being the trainer of the immortal Archer and also Tim Whiffler, first home in 1867. The most highly publicised single bet on behalf of Mr White in 1877 was one of £10,000 to £400 about the 'two Chesters' double with Melbourne's top bookie, the self-titled 'King of the Ring' Joe Thompson. This was a bet recorded with much flair on the cuff of the bookmaker's shirtsleeve and that looked a very nice wager indeed for the politician when Chester prevailed on Derby Day. Adding to Thompson's worries, one of Mr White's friends had backed Chester straight out in the Cup with him to win another £10,000. However, with the money for Savanaka still coming after he ran a fantastic two-mile trial, Mr Power's colt was 4–1 favourite when the Cup field of 1877 jumped, with Mr White's charge at fives.

The racing public was disgusted by the deceptive manner in which the St Albans people had implemented their scheme and were keen to see the favourite go under, and it seemed a number of jockeys shared that view. An unknown lad whose name according to the *Age* was 'Everard' and according to the *Argus* was 'Jerrard' was riding a 100–1 outsider called Waxy, and he appeared particularly keen to keep Savanaka wide. But at the six furlongs, the jockey was so focused on stopping Mr Power's fancy that he didn't see the tearaway leader Fisherman dropping back on top of the field, and Waxy tripped and fell, a calamity that cost the impeded Savanaka a further 20 lengths. At the furlong, Chester kicked well clear and the White camp's bets seemed home, but suddenly a late challenger emerged from the ruck, coming quickly with a powerful burst. It was Savanaka, which dived at the line but missed by half a head, the biggest certainty beaten in Cup history.

Rumours spread that Chester's win had sent Thompson broke, but the bookmaker quickly and proudly announced he would be paying up at 11am the next day, under the verandah of the Hall of Commerce in Collins Street, where speculators usually traded their shares. All and anyone were invited to join him. A gathering of over a thousand spilled out onto the road to see punters paid in gold bars and sovereigns, before Mr White's representative, prominent Sydney lawyer Mr Septimus Stephen, arrived with the English prizefighter Jem Mace, who was touring Australia at the time. 'Jem, accompany me to the bank,' Mr Stephen asked his acclaimed bodyguard, 'and you're on a suit of clothes.' They were there to collect both Mr White's winnings and those of his close friend, and Joe Thompson welcomed the pair warmly before beginning in theatrical fashion to count out his debt in £50 notes. When he reached '400' the crowd roared, and soon after, Stephen and Mace were on their way. The bookmakers paid out plenty that year, but they won plenty, too. Such is the way of the Cup.

De Mestre went on to train a fifth Cup winner, Calamia, the following year and should have had a sixth in 1882, when Sweet William, a heavily backed 4–1 favourite, was kicked at the barrier but still finished fourth on a wet deck behind The Assyrian. That same year, Mr White asked the great trainer to prepare an impressive two-year-old named Martini-Henri, but de Mestre, after advising his esteemed client to give the colt time, decided to wind back his training operations. He suggested his foreman, Michael Fennelly, take over. White and Fennelly set Martini-Henri for a first-up victory in the AJC Derby, but a cough forced the colt's withdrawal, which meant that his debut race would be the Victoria Derby, followed by, if things went to plan, the Cup. White placed a bet of £10,000 to £200 about Martini-Henri in the Melbourne Cup before the AJC Derby, and was convinced to take a further £2000 to £400 about the Victoria Derby and £10,000 to £500 about the Cup in the days leading into the Victorian spring carnival. It seemed incredibly unlikely that a colt could win these two races at its first two starts, but Martini-Henri was up to the challenge. The bookies were skinned again.

It wasn't just the owners of the horses who the bookmakers had to be on guard against. Back in 1889, a horse called Bravo finished third in the Caulfield Cup, but afterwards reports from his stable suggested he had broken down. A respected sporting journalist, Mr AP Morris, was invited to inspect the horse and wrote that a leg was heavily bandaged. Consequently, Bravo eased out to as much as 200–1 for the Melbourne Cup, but — who'd have thought it — he amazingly recovered not long after being sensationally backed in to 8–1. On Cup Day, the favourite, Melos, was repeatedly interfered with but still ran third. Carbine, carrying 10 stone, looked certain to win until his jockey suffered an asthma attack. Meanwhile, the plunge horse enjoyed a perfect run and won by a length. The owners always claimed they didn't support Bravo, but someone did and it wasn't just AP Morris.

Another year when the bookmakers found themselves in real trouble was 1901, when Leslie Macdonald, who had been the racing manager for the late Mr WR Wilson of St Albans fame, discovered that his gelding Revenue had a sensitive wither. Revenue had won the 1899 VRC Sires Produce Stakes for Wilson as a two-year-old, but then lost form. This didn't stop Macdonald from buying him at the St Albans dispersal sale that followed Wilson's death, and when he found the reason why the gelding wasn't giving his best in races he decided to keep him away from race meetings the stable until the weights were announced for the Melbourne Cup. When Revenue was allotted 7.10 for the Cup, Macdonald and his trainer Hugh Munro began backing him quietly with a number of bookmakers at odds around 100–1, and soon they had him running for £60,000. By Cup Day, he was 7–4, then the shortest priced runner in the race's 40-year history.

Not long before the jump, one bookie sidled up to Macdonald and advised the owner to hedge his bets — with him, of course. 'No,' said the owner, 'Revenue shall not be beaten.'

And so it proved. Revenue won by half a length, and that bookmaker was one of a number who had to give the game away for a time.

In 1910, Mr Sol Green's imported stayer Comedy King won the 50th running of the Cup, after connections backed the horse for plenty following a poor run in the Craven Plate in Sydney. Normally, Green liked to paint himself as unlucky, but after Comedy King edged out the favourite, Trafalgar, in a thrilling finish he said quietly, 'This day, I did not lose.'

Green was a Londoner who'd ventured to Australia in 1885 with no money but plenty of cheek and drive. He became a successful bookmaker, with a penchant for Havana cigars and flash cars, and in more recent times developed a magnificent property, 'Underbank', at Bacchus Marsh, 30 miles north-east of Melbourne. This was where Phar Lap spelled over the summer of 1929–30 and again in the winter of 1930. Unfortunately for Sol Green, that now seemed like a long time ago, because on the morning of Derby Day he'd woken up to find his name all over the front page of the Melbourne *Truth*. The story was out that his son Robert had appeared in court after getting himself in trouble financially, and that Dad had been obliged to cover his debts. In court, Bob Green was represented by Mr Robert Menzies KC. If only the Phar Lap shooting had occurred on Friday morning, they all must have thought, that would have kept us off page one.

'So while you might have got good odds about "out of form" horses like Comedy King or Revenue, this year the bookies have never had Phar Lap longer than 6–1 from the time they put up their first markets,' Sullivan explained to Brophy. 'Fancy accepting 6–1 about a horse with 9.12, when there's 300 other horses in the race and months to the jump. Doesn't say much about the rest of them.'

'Says a lot about Phar Lap, though,' Brophy countered.

'He was 4–1 in the middle of August, 3–1 in September. The thing is, we've all got clients we have to look after, and if one of them comes to us and says he wants to back Phar Lap, we let him on. Then it's a matter of trying to lay that bet off, which wasn't easy, but it wasn't impossible either, if that's what you wanted to do.

'Bob Jansen told me that he hardly did any business on the Caulfield Cup. "Practically nothing," he told me, "either straight out or in the doubles. It's a dead letter."'

Jansen was the leader of the Flemington ring, renowned for taking on anyone. On the day he put up his opening markets for the Melbourne Cup back in June he'd been claimed for £6000 to £1000 on Phar Lap straightaway. But that was the only big bet he accepted. After the last on Derby Day, he had Phar Lap at even money, with no takers.

'Connolly's going round claiming that he got 40–1 about the Amounis–Phar Lap double, but that's bunkum,' Sullivan said, in the way a parent talks about a child who never tells the truth. 'Twenty fives at best, but I reckon a fair lump of his bets went on just before Phar Lap was scratched from the Caulfield Cup, when the double was 10–1 and the two Phar Laps was eights. You still could have got 7–4 about Phar Lap to win the Cup last Monday, but most of the bookies who weren't looking pretty snapped that up real quick.'

'Is that what you did?'

'Detective-Sergeant, I might have a whack at Phar Lap on Cup Day, to get some of my money back, or I might let him go and just sink completely if he wins. I'm in so deep I've just got to hope one of the others rescues me, but I'm the only one in that bad. I talked to people like you asked, and while a few of them are going to get thumped if Phar Lap wins, only one of us goes under. That's only the main ring, though. Elsewhere, in the pubs and places like that, I bet a few more will get knocked over, and I guess a few interstate blokes will struggle, too. But I'm your biggest worry. It'll be the worst day of my life if I can't go to settling on Wednesday. You know, I did the sums: they'd have to put two or three thousand quid on Tregilla before I'd bring him in half a point.'

'Tregilla's carrying mine,' Brophy offered sympathetically, as if that would make Sullivan's prospects seem brighter.

'He looks a great chance, your classic Cups three-year-old.' Sullivan responded. 'Take Phar Lap out, and he'd be Revenue's price. It'll be interesting to see what they do at the Call of the Card tomorrow.'

'So you're still going to that?'

'The Call of the Card? Wouldn't miss it.'

This annual Cup-eve event had its origins back in 1880, when a collection of businessmen, lawyers, surgeons, graziers, breeders and other racing enthusiasts formed the 'Victorian Club'. Initially the club premises were in Bourke Street, but soon they moved to Queen Street, where the club became the place where reputable bookmakers and their respected clients settled their bets following major race meetings. The Call of the Card, where the 'caller' would invite the leading bookmakers of the day to quote odds for each horse and punters would say if they were prepared to accept those odds, was always conducted in an atmosphere of much decorum, with cigar smoke wafting through the air. It had become an institution of Cup week, and would always be prominently if carefully reported in the Cup Day editions of the major newspapers, because off-course betting was illegal and the gaming police could have raided the function any year they chose. However, they never did, maybe in part because one of the Victorian Club's founding members had been Captain Standish, the man who had come up with the idea of the Melbourne Cup, a VRC committeeman — and from 1858 to 1880 the Chief Commissioner of the Victoria Police!

'So, Sam, let's get this straight. Are you telling me the bookmakers didn't shoot Phar Lap?' Brophy asked.

'No, I can't say that for sure. Some unlicensed bookies are crooked and crooks'll be crooks. It might just be one bird trying to save his skin. But I can tell you for sure that the shooting was not some conspiracy among us because we're all about to be wiped out. You're barking up the wrong tree trying to get anywhere with that one.'

THE PHONE HAD BEEN ringing hot all day at Joe Cripps' place, and all day Harry Telford had been refusing to take calls from anyone other than his closest friends. However, around 7pm, Bert Wolfe was on the phone again, and Telford relented. After all, Bert was a good bloke, the kind of journo who never gave up a source or betrayed a trust, and Phar Lap's harried trainer knew 'Cardigan' would be happy with a couple of quotes on the record and then they could have a chat, racing man to racing man.

'Phar Lap will win the Melbourne Cup without an effort,' Telford said down the phone after they'd exchanged greetings. 'Some people who know that he is a good thing for the race have become desperate in their attempt to prevent him from getting to the post. The public can be assured that I will take no risk of anyone doing damage to the horse between now and the time that he steps on the course at Flemington.'

'You weren't there when they tried to get him, were you, Harry?' Wolfe asked.

'When the attempt was made to shoot Phar Lap I was still at the course. I knew nothing of the matter until told by my men.'

'And what precautions are you taking now?'

'It will be difficult to get at the horse in a similar manner again. From now until Tuesday I am going to shift him from the stables to the course and home again in a motor float.'

'That'll do it, Harry. Thanks mate. How are you holding up?'

'Jeez, I'll be glad when it's over, Bert.' You could sense Telford's disposition change. 'Fair dinkum, the pressure is killing me. Tuesday can't come quick enough.'

CHAPTER ELEVEN

BLUEY AND BRADMAN

GUY RAYMOND HADN'T BACKED Phar Lap, and had no intention of backing Phar Lap. When the story of the champion's getaway was eventually told, it would win some good publicity for the stud and perhaps doing the right thing by the Cup favourite might win him some favour if he stood for the VRC Committee next year. But as he fidgeted around outside Phar Lap's temporary home in the middle of the night, his old army revolver in his pocket, he wasn't motivated by such thoughts. A bit of it was the hero thing, and there always the obligation to do the right thing, but most of it was the thrill of being on the 'front line'. Just as Woodcock had shown courage beyond the call of duty when he positioned himself between Phar Lap and the gunman in the Studebaker, so too, in a sense, was Raymond, as he stood watch through a warm Sunday night and into early Monday morning. If the gangsters knew where the horse was residing, the owner of St Alban's Stud might be stranded.

As it turned out, the dark held no drama, and when Woodcock roused early to take the horse for a prolonged walk, Raymond insisted on coming along for the first couple of miles. When he learned that Phar Lap liked a fuss being made of him while he was feeding, Raymond hung around — and even thought himself personally responsible when the gelding cleaned out his bin. A little later, Woodcock was asked if he'd seen anyone spying on him when he took Phar Lap around the paddocks.

'No, not a soul,' he responded.

'I didn't either,' Raymond said quickly, explaining that he'd had his field glasses on his two important guests all the time, just to make sure everything was okay. 'I had my rifle by my side, too, and would have used it if necessary.' Some might have thought such behaviour unnecessarily dramatic; Woodcock reckoned it was wonderful. He'd felt comfortable with Mr Raymond from the moment they met.

BACK AT CAULFIELD, HARRY Telford's plan was to use Phar Lap's stablemate Old Ming as a double for the Cup favourite at trackwork on Monday morning, and it was working perfectly until he actually ran into someone. Telford had dressed the two-year-old filly in one of Phar Lap's rugs — she was a chestnut and big for her age, though not as tall as her famous stablemate — and bandaged her front legs, they had a constable for company, and Stan Boyden even picked them up at Beverley Street and drove them to Caulfield's back gate. But no sooner had 'Phar Lap' been offloaded and a passing trainer quietly said, 'Not galloping Phar Lap this morning, Harry?' A strapper asked, 'You given Tommy the morning off, Mr Telford?' Then a reporter from the *Judge*, who'd been waiting for them near the entrance, rushed up and asked, 'Is there something amiss with Phar Lap? Why isn't he here?'

'None of your business,' the trainer grizzled. Soon he and Jack Martin were walking over to the infield, and then they saw all the reporters awaiting his arrival.

'Well, this is all going just terrific,' Telford mumbled to himself.

A fair crowd had gathered over near the grandstand, all of them there to watch Phar Lap work. There was no option but to continue with the charade, and Old Ming ran a few furlongs in what was good style for her, not so good for whom she was supposed to be. Ideally, Telford would have liked to get out of there as quickly as he could, but one of the stablehands had brought up two more of his team (in all, he had seven horses, not counting Phar Lap, at Joe Cripps' place) and Telford had a duty to watch them.

So watch them he did. In silence. All media inquiries were ignored. Eventually, one of the local horsemen walked over, and the two engaged in conversation for maybe a minute, before Telford said, 'Righto, good to see you, gotta go,' and he was on his way. In an instant, the press converged on the fellow who'd gone over for a chat, and gleaned only that Phar Lap had been taken to 'an unknown destination'. The chestnut, it seemed, did not need another serious gallop before the Cup, but 'suitable arrangements' had been made to get him the necessary exercise away from prying eyes and errant shotguns. That was all the reporters had to take back to their editors.

'WE NEVER DID DISCOVER who found those pellets, did we?' Jack Brophy asked Harold Saker at CIB Headquarters early on Monday morning. 'We know now. First, though, have a look at the *Sun News-Pictorial*.'

Brophy handed over the paper, which had a big story on page three headlined: 'PELLETS FOUND IN FENCE AT

CAULFIELD'. The sub-heading to the report was 'Gun Fired At Phar Lap On Way Back From Early Morning Track Work'. In many ways, it seemed incongruous that the discovery of the pellets was more newsworthy than the shooting itself. There was no mention in the story of who might have found this evidence.

'Now, what do you think of the *Argus*?' Brophy inquired of his partner. That paper's story was headlined 'SHOT FIRED AT PHAR LAP', and halfway down the column, under the small heading of 'Pellets Found', was the following:

A theory in some quarters that the incident was a stunt and that a blank cartridge was fired was disproved when Mr J. Bird, racehorse trainer of Manchester Grove, Caulfield, found near the fence against where Phar Lap had been led, the cardboard wad from the cartridge. In it were marks made by the leaden pellets. Mr Bird made a mark on the fence near where he found the wad. He was unable to find any pellets or any marks where pellets had struck the fence. Yesterday morning, however, Mr W.J. Hall of Queens Avenue, Caulfield, the track representative of 'The Argus', found several No. 6 pellets on the footpath about 6 yards nearer James Street and others were found embedded in the fence ...

From the moment the name 'Mr W.J. Hall' jumped out of the page, the two detectives were thinking exactly the same thing: they were being played for mugs. The situation they'd discovered the previous day at Etna Street had been strange, almost bizarre, in the sense that things that had not been there one day had miraculously appeared the next. Quite clearly, someone had decided that the crime scene needed dressing up. Whether it was Hall who planted the pellets, or whether Hall simply got lucky after they'd been left by someone else, was still to be resolved. Hall and James Creed, another track watcher, were both now significant witnesses in this investigation; was it too ridiculous to speculate that they might actually be more than mere bystanders? If the pellets had come from the shotgun there should have been at least 100 of them in the fence and there weren't. Nothing like it. Maybe the pellets in the tree branch and the fence had been punched in with a hammer.

The *Age*'s report was very specific when it came to the number of pellets found at the scene:

> Definite evidence of the attempted shooting was obtained by Detective Sergeant Brophy and Detective H.G. Saker when they made a search of the scene of the outrage Saturday morning. Embedded in a cypress tree they recovered two shot-gun pellets. Five pellets and a cartridge cap were also found on the footpath close to the fence. The detectives expressed the opinion that the charge was fired about three feet six inches off the ground, and at an angle of 45 deg. The object of the men, they said, was to wound Phar Lap in the flanks, and so injure him that he would have to be withdrawn from the Melbourne Cup ...

'What should we do?' Saker wondered. He was thinking that perhaps they could get Bill Hall in a darkened room so they could explain to him exactly how taxed the limited resources of the CIB were at the moment.

Brophy, in contrast, seemed fairly relaxed about it all. 'Go and see him, Harold, but I reckon unless we hear something from Geelong, the status quo will do me,' he said. 'I've got a job to do for General Blamey. There's a summons needs delivering this afternoon to the Police Association Secretary.'

'Won't the press be into you for worrying about the union when you should be saving Phar Lap?' Saker asked.

'The Commissioner asked to be kept informed about Phar Lap and that's exactly what I'll do when I see him,' Brophy said. 'For the moment, if someone wants to muck us around, we'll just keep our eyes open and play along. Don't forget, there are people out there who don't want Phar Lap to run. But if we can keep the bookies out there as the prime suspects for long enough, you'll be able to get into the Call of the Card tonight, we'll get plum seats for the Cup tomorrow, and maybe we can get this thing worked out in a way where no one gets hurt.'

COMMISSIONER BLAMEY HAD BEEN in dispute with the Victorian Police Association from just about the day he first took office in 1925. His free-market ideology was in stark contrast to that of the trade union, and he chose as a key point of difference the matter of policemen being promoted on merit rather than seniority. He wanted officers put to a test before they were appointed to higher-ranking jobs, with he, the Commissioner, having the final power to reject or accept recommendations from district superintendents. The Association, believing Blamey's primary motivation was to get men of his own kind in senior positions, would have none of it. In early 1929, it seemed certain that Sir William McPherson's conservative government would introduce regulations supporting Blamey's concept, but by November a Labor administration had assumed office and the implementation of the new rules was postponed. Instead, Premier Edmond Hogan announced that Blamey's re-appointment as Commissioner when his term expired on September 1, 1930, which had been considered a *fait accompli*, would be reviewed.

Blamey was retained, but on lower pay and with a three-year

contract in his pocket rather than the customary five. He'd show them, and three days into his second term he made his move against the Association. Because the General Secretary, one Victor Price, was not a police officer, Crown Solicitor Frank Menzies, brother of Robert, had advised that the Association was an improperly constituted body. Price had been General Secretary for 12 months. Section 81, subsection 2 of the Police Regulations Act stated the association was to be 'entirely independent and unassociated with any body or persons outside the force', but whether having a civilian in what was essentially a senior administrative role made the whole union operation illegal was open to interpretation. Menzies' predecessor as Crown Solicitor had never had a problem. Regardless, the Association wrote to the Chief Secretary, via Blamey, offering to amend its constitution to fix the matter, but Blamey refused to pass on the letter. Instead, he issued an order through the *Victorian Police Gazette* to members of the force that they should disassociate themselves forthwith from what was now deemed an illegal union. Six days later, Price countered with a circular to all members, which began:

Dear Comrade,

No doubt, you and those stationed in your district have seen and very probably freely discussed the notice issued in the Gazette by the Chief Commissioner of Police concerning the future activities of the Association.

Just what will be the outcome of this contemplated action I am not in a position to say at present. At all events, it is not as black as it looks.

Now there is one other point I want to stress very forcibly, and that is this — On no account must the members of your district resign from this Association.

The reason for this is that even if you have to reconstruct the Association and have a member of the force as Secretary, do not let the little coterie of men at Russell Street have matters all their own way ...

Price argued that he was defending the rights of his Association; Blamey reckoned he was inducing officers to disobey an order from the Commissioner, and that was a criminal offence. So on October 20, Blamey asked one of his favourite detective-sergeants at Russell Street to go to the Association's offices in Swanston Street, to interview Price, in essence to gather evidence with a view to laying charges. Brophy was down there like a shot.

Two weeks later, at 11am sharp, he was outside Blamey's office, waiting for the appropriately autographed summons that was to be handed to Price and at the same time trying to decide exactly what the Commissioner needed to know about Phar Lap. Brophy now had absolutely no doubt that the gunman had been firing blanks. The men in the Studebaker might have really been trying to scare and thus stop the horse from running in the Cup, but if that was right, they weren't very good at it and they certainly weren't the bloodthirsty operators the underworld would have employed to perform such a dastardly deed. When it came to the shooting it wasn't Al Capone he was dealing with here, more like Al Jolson or Alice in bloody Wonderland.

When, after handing him the relevant paperwork, the Commissioner said, 'Detective-Sergeant, when you get back, let me know how you got on', Brophy decided that as far as Phar Lap was concerned, he'd bought himself some time. He didn't bring the subject up and, surprisingly, neither did Blamey.

The Police Association's offices were a short walk south of police headquarters, and Brophy took the long way. He met his partner on the case against the Association Secretary, Detective-Sergeant Mick Davey, on the corner of Russell and Lonsdale Streets, before climbing up to the second floor of the Association's building, where he saw Price for long enough to say the expected things and hand him an envelope. Then it was back to Russell Street, where he went not to his own office, nor to the Commissioner's suite, but to see Inspector Fred Piggott, his partner from the infamous Gun Alley atrocity. Piggott was a stylish, always immaculately dressed officer who never swore, a straight shooter whose opinion Brophy respected. The two were hardly good mates, different in so many ways and very much on different sides of the Police Association controversy, but they respected each other's work and Gun Alley had inevitably forged a bond between them. As much as anything, it had taught them both about the media's influence in modern police work. It had been Squizzy Taylor, no less, who'd once written to the *Herald* to declare, among other things:

> For the old saying goes ...
> Ashes to ashes, dust to dust;
> if Brophy don't get you,
> well, Piggott must.

Soon Brophy and Piggott were joined by the head of the CIB, Superintendent Walsh, and Brophy outlined the evidence about the Phar Lap shooting (or lack thereof) and his concern that members of the press might have become players rather than just reporters. All three men were fully aware of the public relations battle the force had got itself involved in with the press, how the papers had latched onto the question of whether the people of Victoria had an efficient and effective police service. It'd be nice to tag them with something like this, to keep them quiet for a while, but on the other hand, now was not the time to be falsely accusing the media of deception. So the trio resolved to sit quiet for a little longer, maybe even until after the Cup had been run and won.

THE DISCOVERY OF PELLETS at Etna Street and the rumours that Phar Lap's whereabouts were unknown ensured there was great anticipation when the first edition of the *Herald* hit the streets. Police Headquarters' copy landed first on Brophy's desk, and he saw immediately that the major stories were both sporting ones. Over in columns six and seven, under the headline 'Test Cricketers Receive Warm Welcome' was a report on the Ashes squad's arrival at Port Melbourne that morning, complete with a smiling headshot of 'Test team hero' Don Bradman, even though he wasn't there when captain Bill Woodfull and his men disembarked. However, the dominant page-one news was of the Cup, which spread over columns one, two, three and half of column four ...

100,000 EXPECTED AT MELBOURNE CUP TOMORROW

Course in Excellent Condition
PHAR LAP IN HIDING UNTIL BIG EVENT TAKES PLACE
Cool Weather Predicted

Australia's most important racing week of the year will reach its zenith tomorrow, when Cup Day will be celebrated at Flemington by, it is estimated, 100,000 people.

The day will be a close holiday throughout the State.

The weather forecast issued at noon today for the ensuing 24 hours says:

At first, windy, warm and sultry, with freshening northerly wind but followed tonight by a squally, south-westerly change with cool, cloudy, squally and unsettled to showery weather tomorrow.

Phar Lap, the favorite for the Melbourne Cup, is 'in hiding' and very few people know where he is spending his final hours before he runs in the Melbourne Cup.

The Herald Turf Writer's final selections for the Cup are:

1. Phar Lap
2. Tregilla
3. Balloon King
4. Soulton

The first race at Flemington — the Cup Hurdle — is timed for 1pm. Hours before that, however, ardent speculators with a fancy for picking doubles — and even trebles — at outside prices by getting in early, and family parties to whom a picnic on the Hill is almost as great an attraction as the Cup itself, will be winding their way to the world's best racecourse.

The race for the Cup — one almost writes Phar Lap's Cup, so highly fancied is the favorite — will start at 3.30pm and about three and a half minutes later the result will be known throughout the Commonwealth ...

In column two was a story headlined 'Guarding Phar Lap For The Cup', which included the information that 'early on Sunday morning he was placed in a float and driven to an unknown destination'. But that was all; six lines later the reporter was describing the Old Ming subterfuge that had fooled no one. Telford was not quoted. But underneath the story were three photographs, rather dramatically headed: 'Guarding Phar Lap: Today's Pictures'.

The first, largest photograph was of two pellets embedded in the fence, complete with the *Herald* reporter's index finger. Below it was a shot of a constable standing guard outside Cripps' stables. And the third shot was a close-up of 'Bluey', Harry Telford's fiery blue cattle dog, with his muzzle off. It was the same size as the Bradman headshot.

FOR WOODCOCK, RAYMOND AND Parker at the 'unknown destination', nothing much was happening, which was perfect. Telford had left instructions with Woodcock to gallop Phar Lap only if he thought it necessary. They'd decided that the trainer would stay away from St Alban's until Tuesday morning, the logic being that by keeping his distance he'd put the gangsters off the scent. The downside was that he lost control of the horse's preparation so close to their biggest day, but his horseman's instinct told him that the unique bond between Phar Lap and Woodcock was something that might work in their favour. It had in the past.

Telford was from the old school, where work and more work was needed to get a stayer equipped for a two-mile race; Woodcock was a gentler soul who thought if you talked nicely enough to a good horse then it'd do just about anything you asked of it. Raymond, who was on the Geelong Racing Club's committee, had explained that he could take them down to the local racecourse for a private gallop, but Woodcock was happier taking his mate for another walk. This one, straight after lunch, was briefer than the morning, only three miles, most of it around and around the training track. All the while, Raymond had his glasses peeled, and when around two o'clock he saw something strange gathering on the northwestern horizon, he dashed out to suggest that Tommy take Bobby back to his stall. But it was only Mother Nature. A huge dust cloud was sweeping down from Central Australia — it had already swamped towns such as Broken Hill, Swan Hill, Mildura, Echuca, Ballarat and Bendigo — and would soon be turning Geelong's vivid blue afternoon sky an eerie orange red.

MELBOURNE WAS COVERED IN dust not long after Geelong. Among those caught up in it were the hundreds of unemployed who'd converged on the city for a march to the government offices in Spring Street. Brophy was there, too, discreetly surveying the scene, staying long enough to hear the veteran Labor member for Footscray, former premier George Prendergast, complain to the mob that more than 200,000 people were now unemployed in Victoria. Prendergast also blurted through the loudspeaker that the only reason they'd been able to march in peace on this occasion was because the police had left them alone for a change, not provoking trouble like they usually do. He put that down to the fact it was Cup week and the authorities didn't want a scene with all the visitors about. Brophy nodded; there was more than a hint of truth in that.

On the way back, he ducked into a hotel on Flinders Street, near the Herald and Weekly Times building, not for a pot of beer but for a quiet chat with the publican, a good and trusted ally who occasionally picked up information about what the crime reporters were doing. It was rarely a shock for Brophy to find out that the press knew more than he did. They were better resourced, after all.

'Have you found the Phar Lap killers yet, Jack?' the publican asked.

'No, they haven't poked their heads up yet. Don't know if they ever will.'

'It's funny, I thought I'd found them for you,' drawled the hotel owner as he slowly applied a towel to a recently washed glass.

'What do you mean,' Brophy's curiosity had been aroused.

'Last Thursday arvo I overheard a few newspaper types talking the idea up. Seemed to me they were planning to have some fun with all the frenzy about the horse. You know, fire some blanks, cause a scene. They were having a right ol' laugh about it. Until you found those pellets in the fence I thought they'd actually followed through.'

'Mate, are you fair dinkum?' Brophy asked, trying to sound earnest rather than incredulous. 'Can you keep that to yourself?'

'I don't think that'll be too hard, Jack. I told a couple of blokes about it on Saturday night and they just laughed at me. I'd have had more chance convincing 'em Squizzy Taylor did it!'

The idea that reporters would build up the image of the hoods in the Studebaker and then embellish the crime scene for their own benefit was one thing. The idea they'd concoct the whole sorry story was something else. Maybe the fact that a single pellet-riddled *newspaper* had suddenly appeared at Etna Street on the Sunday morning was more revealing than it had appeared. By the time Brophy returned to his office it was a quarter past three, his mind was racing, and he found Saker pacing near his door, a small, torn piece of newsprint and a somewhat crumpled envelope in his hand. Brophy, of course, had his own information to reveal, but Saker was keen to first provide news of his meeting with Bill Hall, who he'd found at his home in Caulfield at lunchtime, at first appearing very pleased with himself that he had been the man to find the missing pellets. However, then he'd had it explained to him that because his discovery confirmed beyond doubt that a shot had been fired, the investigation was no longer simply about frightening a horse, it was a case of shooting at a strapper. Hall's mood quickly changed, especially after Saker refused to say 'no' when the track representative asked if that meant he was a suspect.

'Did you plant those pellets on Sunday morning?' Saker asked.

'No.'

'Did someone tell you they were there?'

'Might have.'

'Who might have?'

'Ah, not sure, really. It was an anonymous tip-off.'

'Come off it, Hall, you're a track watcher, not a bloody crime reporter. Name me one member of the underworld who's got you in his telephone book?'

Soon after, Hall conceded that he had overheard reporters at Caulfield on Sunday morning talking about the news that no pellets had been found, and decided off his own bat to go down to the corner of James and Etna to have a good look for himself. There the pellets were, so when the real pressmen arrived soon after, he was quick to put his hand up as the man who found them.

Now Brophy could tell of his conversation at the pub. 'So you reckon they did the driving and the shotgun themselves?' Saker reacted.

'I don't know for sure. Like we've said, it wouldn't be hard to find a motor, a driver and a gun if they thought it was a fun idea but weren't game to do it themselves. But most people these days can drive and shoot straight.'

'Jack, they didn't need someone to shoot straight!'

The detectives sniggered wearily at the lousy joke. Maybe it didn't really matter who the culprits were. 'What've you got there, Harold?' Brophy asked, looking at the envelope in his partner's hand.

'Another warning letter,' Saker had almost forgotten what he was holding. 'I think Walsh wanted you to see it because of who it was addressed to.'

On the envelope was a name and address, written in extravagant longhand:

To South Eastern District
Det. Sgt. Piggot
Police Headquarters
Russell St
City
Urgent

It had been post-marked at 4.30 that morning, at the city's main post office. The stamp on it was fixed upside down, a recognised sign of distress, and it had found its way to Piggott's desk by 3pm, and then, quickly, via superintendents Fitzgerald and Walsh, to the attention of Saker and Brophy. On the newsprint, in blue pencil and in the same longhand script, was the following message:

To Mr Piggot
　　Just to inform you and to warn you to have your men ready to avoid bad smash on cup day.
　　Phar Lap and Amounis will be shot during the running of the race that they are in.
　　Have your men along the rails back of course.
　　Leading Bookmakers on the rails and flat are paying for this job.

The letter was signed: 'One that Knows'.

The warning itself was spurious. Amounis would be home in his stable on Cup Day, and anyone with even a beginner's knowledge of the turf knew that. Furthermore, police stations across Melbourne had been getting warning letters and phone calls like this about Phar Lap and what was going to happen to him pretty consistently since word had first got out about the shooting. Most of them had been filed in the rubbish bin.

However, this one was now very different. On the back of the sheet on which the warning had been written, in big red letters, were the A, L and D of the word 'HERALD'. The piece of cheap paper on which the writer had chosen to send his message was from the top right-hand corner of a *Herald* poster that would normally have sat outside a newsagent or newsstand, letting potential readers know about the day's major story. Had it come from two days ago, it would have carried news of the Phar Lap shooting. However, it was impossible to tell what news the poster had been headlining, because the piece torn off to carry the warning had been quite deliberately ripped to feature just the last three letters of the name of Melbourne's leading evening paper.

To Jack Brophy, given what they had been discovering over the past two-and-a-half days, and especially what he'd heard at the pub in the past half-hour, this was akin to a confession. This crude, brief note and the small envelope in which it came were going into the official police file. While he and Saker weren't prepared to accept that the perpetrators were from the *Herald* — they might be, sure, but they might just as easily be people from the other papers, trying to pin one on that mob, and it wasn't as if only 'HWT' employees drank at that Flinders Street pub — but enough things now pointed to a press beat-up.

Were the culprits racing writers or 'regular' reporters? You'd have to start with the blokes who knew how and when Phar Lap went to Caulfield for trackwork, Brophy quickly thought to himself, but then he realised that this sort of information wouldn't be hard to discover. This was also the turf writers' busiest time of the year. They hardly had time to be planning elaborate hoaxes. On top of that, almost to a man they truly loved their sport and wouldn't do anything to hurt any horse, let alone a true champion like Phar Lap. Saker was sure both Creed and Hall fitted this description. The detectives did agree that it was certainly possible that Creed had been exploited — that the Studebaker was parked in a place that the miscreants knew was on his regular route to Caulfield racecourse. Hall was probably simply lucky to be the one to find the pellets. Maybe the idea was that the police were supposed to make that critical discovery, but the track watcher had got there first.

Should they get a gang of reporters in for a chat, or was there a better way? Brophy and Saker had to remember that even if the shooting was a prank, there was still a real danger to Phar Lap while it was possible by fair means or foul to stop that damn Cups double coming true. Pragmatism was more important than procedure.

Brophy looked again at the envelope, at how it was addressed: to 'Det. Sgt. Piggot'. Back in 1922, Brophy, Piggott and the Herald had made their names through the resolution of the Gun Alley murder. How ironic it would be, Brophy thought, if another case in which he was involved might now besmirch the newspaper's reputation.

CHAPTER TWELVE

THE CALL OF THE CARD

A MELBOURNE BARRISTER NAMED Harry Alderman once said to General Blamey, 'You know, Tom, you have to be a very innocent man to buck the press.'

Blamey's reply was typically blunt: 'I am not afraid of the press.'

Which was probably just as well, because the papers hadn't been kind to him during the past five years. Consequently, when Superintendent Walsh and Detective-Sergeant Brophy started explaining to him how they believed the press had set up the Phar Lap shooting and were now exploiting that deception to sell their papers, the Commissioner quickly became very excited, like a batsman who'd finally found proof that the umpire really is a cheat.

'Do you know which paper, Detective-Sergeant?'

'No, sir,' Brophy responded as he handed Blamey the crumpled letter detailing the latest threat to Phar Lap and Amounis, 'Looking at this, maybe it's the *Herald*. Or maybe someone's trying to convince us it's the *Herald*.'

'The *Herald*, eh? Perhaps I should go and have a word with Mr Murdoch,' Blamey said. 'No, that would not work. Even if his paper was involved, he would call my bluff. I will have to talk to the editors of all the papers. Should I point out that if we find the perpetrators they will be facing an attempted murder charge? Gentlemen, that is what I should do. Please keep me informed if anything develops.'

Keith Murdoch's career had progressed most handsomely since the days of Gun Alley, when the paper's extensive coverage of Brophy and Piggott's murder investigation and the subsequent trial and execution of Colin Ross led to an almost doubling of its circulation. Murdoch was now the managing director of the 'Herald and Weekly Times', the media company that controlled a string of newspapers in Victoria and South Australia, including the *Herald*, the *Sun News-Pictorial*, the *Weekly Times*, *Sporting Globe*, *Table Talk*, the Adelaide *Register* and Adelaide *Advertiser*, plus Melbourne radio station 3DB. He and Blamey went back to the War — both had been at Gallipoli, though not at the same time, and their paths crossed from time to time in the three years afterwards, on the Western Front and in London. While they did not become close associates, they did, independently and proudly, develop a strong faith in the Australian spirit, and belief in the viability and importance of the Australian Army.

Murdoch's journalistic philosophy was to exploit the sensation of the day for all it was worth. No one was above criticism or scrutiny if it would increase sales, even if he was the Chief Commissioner of Police. Blamey was a soldier who believed that with rank came privileges. The *Herald* would have none of that. Blamey loved the 'sport of kings', whereas Murdoch was not a racing man, even if his father-in-law, Mr Rupert Greene, was the official VRC starter. To Keith Murdoch, Phar Lap was not so much a champion horse as a prominent name in a headline.

At the other end of the newspaper spectrum from the *Herald* and the *Sun News-Pictorial* was the *Age*. In days gone by, with the legendary David Syme at the helm, this paper had been known as the 'Thunderer', but after Mr Syme's death in 1908, ownership had passed to his children, with the eldest, Herbert, running the business and the fourth son, Geoffrey, in charge of editorial. Nowadays, the *Age* was as conservative as they come, resisting any move to sensationalise the news and in the process losing substantial ground to the Herald & Weekly Times publications. In between Murdoch and the Syme family was the *Argus*, Melbourne's third major morning paper. Blamey had contacts in senior places at all three organisations and while these newspapermen weren't always kind to him at least they would listen when he called.

'If it is the papers,' Blamey said to Walsh and Brophy, 'I don't want anyone to know.'

A little later, when Saker asked what the Commissioner was likely to say to the newspaper chiefs, Brophy shrugged his shoulders. 'They'll have an amiable enough chat,' he said. 'General Blamey will raise the matter of the shooting. The paper men will react indignantly — I can imagine Murdoch being horrified by the very idea of a reporter forging the news — and we'll back off, asking only that they look into it.'

'And that'll be it?' asked Saker. 'What do we do then?'

'We have a look at the papers first thing in the morning. If we're right, there'll be nothing in them about the shooting, or maybe just a single paragraph buried somewhere inside, and after that nothing. An order will go out to kill the story, no questions asked, and we'll have to be happy with that. The *Herald* might not even mention the incident in their Cup coverage tomorrow arvo. By Wednesday, the story will be forgotten.'

'What about the blokes who did it? Do we go after them?'

'No, we'll never find out who they are. They'll learn one way or another that if they breathe a word of what they did to anyone, they'll be out of a job. And one thing you don't want to be these days is unemployed. They'll also be led to believe that we really are keen to up the ante to attempted murder. The Cup'll be over and the shooting will suffer a quick and natural death. Years from now, when a reporter tries to claim that he was involved, no one will believe him. The bookies will have to cop the blame forever.'

'What if we're wrong? What if the papers had nothing to do with it?'

'You'll still be reading about the shooting and how we're bungling the investigation for the next week or more. We'll have to find ourselves some gunmen and the bookmaker who was behind it. Poor old Sam Sullivan might be in more trouble than he knows.'

THE SPORTING JUDGE WAS Melbourne's second biggest-selling racing paper, after the *Sporting Globe*. It took a more cynical, irreverent approach to its coverage than the *Globe*, and believed its principal purpose was to give punters as much information as it possibly could. After the Caulfield Cup, one of its columnists had been prepared to write, 'Some of the thinkers are still of the opinion more than one horse was not out to beat Amounis.' When news of the Phar Lap shooting came to light, the *Judge* saw it as its duty to print up a special one-page report, which was distributed to punters through city outlets and at the track on the Saturday afternoon. For its special Melbourne Cup edition, which hit the streets on the afternoon of Cup eve, the paper had gathered no less than 144 different tips for the big race — from prominent bookmakers, trainers, jockeys, owners, administrators, even high-profile racing administrators such as LKS Mackinnon.

Among the 84 who went for Phar Lap was Mr WS Hickenbotham, son of the late Walter Hickenbotham, trainer of the immortal Carbine as well as other Cup winners Mentor (1888), Newhaven (1896) and Blue Spec (1905), who stated that the basis for his selection was that 'Phar Lap was a better horse than Carbine'. Harry Telford claimed his champion was a 'certainty', while David Davis said, 'I have no fear of my horse being beaten, unless someone puts a bullet in him.' Among the 34 who tipped Tregilla were notables such as Ned Moss, Eric Connolly and Jim Scobie, a man who'd trained four Melbourne Cup winners. The great jockey Billy Duncan was another Tregilla supporter. 'I don't remember having seen a horse run as well as Tregilla did at Moonee Valley,' he said of the colt's Cox Plate finish. Of course, the *Judge* was not the only paper to provide such tips, they just had more of them, but it had to be noted that some experts, Sol Green being one example, gave new meaning to the term 'each way bet' by tipping Phar Lap in some papers and Tregilla in others.

JOHN WREN HADN'T BEEN to the Call of the Card for a few years, but most people weren't surprised to see him there in 1930, as he did have a horse, Muratti, engaged in the Cup. Still, such was his reputation around Melbourne, there was a buzz in the room as he was shown to his seat by Mr Frank Shillabeer, the chairman of the Victorian Club. Mr Shillabeer was as interested in this Call as was Mr Wren, for he was the owner of the Moonee Valley Cup winner Shadow King.

One of Melbourne's most prominent builders, a former city councillor and mayor of Footscray, Shillabeer was a short rotund fellow and a man of enormous enterprise. Before Shadow King, his best horses had been jumpers, most notably Sandule, the Grand National Hurdle champion of 1920. For years he raced his horses under the glamorous nom de plume of 'Monckton Franklin', his yellow, pink sleeves, black cap colours became extremely familiar around the city racetracks, and his great ambition was to own the winner of a cup, any cup. Now that Shadow King had done that job for him at Moonee Valley, he was setting his sights much higher, even though his trainer, Ted Fisher, was not keen to start the gelding again in a two-mile handicap. Having finished a tired sixth in the 1929 Melbourne Cup after winning the Hotham Handicap, and having been penalised six pounds this year for his Moonee Valley Cup win, few gave him much hope of conquering Phar Lap.

Mr Shillabeer had bittersweet memories of one of Shadow King's first trips to the racetrack, but at least they gave him hope that an upset wasn't impossible. As a two-year-old, Shadow King was entered in a race at Moonee Valley, but was so disturbed by the experience that Fisher had to tie him tight in his stall, so he wouldn't bolt away. The headstrong colt hated this restraint, and struggled so hard to overcome the rope he was in a muck lather when it finally came time to go to the saddling paddock. Fisher wanted to scratch him, but the owner decided, seeing they were already here, to let the horse run.

Mr Norman Falkiner, a close friend of Mr Shillabeer, had a colt running in the same race, which he considered to be a certainty and the two men backed it into a very short quote. In the straight, Mr Falkiner's colt dashed clear, and the men thought they had their money, when — of all horses! — Shadow King charged down the outside to knock them out. At least Mr Shillabeer had the consolation of knowing he owned an above-average performer.

Whether he was good enough to beat Phar Lap was another matter entirely. At the Victorian Club, a long table ran for most of the length of the 'settling room' — where the day after the Cup bookmakers and punters would return to honour, or as it is said, 'settle' their bets. As the Call of the Card drew closer, the bookies took their seats along either side of that table. At the table's head was the 'caller' and standing around the room were the punters in their hundreds, many in dinner suits, top hats left at the cloak room. This year, many of those top hats were spattered in orange, for following the dust storm that had blanketed the city in the late afternoon it had started to rain, 'red rain'. Now, outside, booming cracks of thunder could be heard, a gale was howling and the flickers of lightning through the gloom gave the evening an exotic eerie mood.

Only Victorian Club members or friends of members were invited, but still the crowd spilled out into the foyer and up the staircase. Many men were attending the event before joining their wives for another Cup-eve function. The caller would name a horse, starting with the topweight, and then ask the bookmakers for their price. The punters might take the best odds nominated or ask for more. More often than not, the bookmakers would accommodate them if their initial quote was unacceptable; occasionally there'd be no business at all. In years gone by, business could be frantic with horses backed for tens of thousands of pounds in a matter of minutes. Fortunes were won or lost.

This time, the anticipation was enormous, because everyone believed that there were at least one or two bookmakers who needed to back Phar Lap at any price to get their ledgers in a semblance of order. Right on half-past six, the caller announced,

'Phar Lap, what price?' A bookie offered 'six to four' and two of his comrades went whack! '£1500 to £1000!' And the 6-4 was gone. Almost immediately: '£1100 to £800!' Then, '£1000 to £800!' and '£500 to £400!' no less than eight times. '£250 to £200!' four times. All up, Phar Lap was backed to win around £10,000, which to veteran observers wasn't really very much at all. Call of the Card veterans had seen favourites backed to win 20 times this amount. In 1930, too many of the bookmakers simply couldn't afford to take the favourite on.

Not surprisingly, many punters didn't like being forced to take such a short price about their Cup selection, no matter how confident they might have been. The Melbourne Cup was a handicap, and handicaps are supposed to be open affairs. Harold Saker had found a spot in the settling room, squeezed up against the wall. 'Even money!' the gentleman at his shoulder cried, as those in the crowd keen to punt tried to cajole the bookmakers into being more generous. 'It's a ridiculous price! Didn't they see last year's Cup? He couldn't get two mile with 7.6, how will he get it with 9.12?'

From nearby, another pundit shouted, 'How many horses have won the Craven Plate–Melbourne Cup double in the past 30 years? One, Windbag! How many have done the Melbourne Stakes–Cup double? Two, Malua and Carbine! What about the Victoria Derby as a three-year-old, then the Cup the year after? Never! Not in 68 years! Same with the AJC Derby. Even money is ridiculous!'

These facts were true. Phar Lap was trying to complete all these doubles. Saker was caught up in the atmosphere; the room was packed with a wealth of racing acumen. And he sensed that if any more 5-4 became available, this man next to him would be trying his utmost to get on. To the uninitiated, it was absurd how at 5-4 Phar Lap was value, at evens he was too short. But in reality this reflected just how important it was for those struggling to balance the books to get the very best price they could. Maybe there would be some 5–4 available at the track.

Eventually, it was time for the horse that would carry the No. 2 saddlecloth, the veteran stayer Donald, to be called. There was a little interest at triple figure odds, nothing at 80s. 'Not surprised,' Saker's new friend advised flatly. 'He might have won a couple of Summer Cups in Sydney and a Newcastle Cup, but a nine-year-old has never won the Melbourne Cup.'

Even less inviting was Mr Lee Steere's moody galloper Second Wind, which after his poor run in the Hotham on Saturday could generate no more than 10 separate bets of £500 to £4. Back in March he'd been beaten 20 lengths by Phar Lap over two miles at Flemington but at least in the Cup he'd met Telford's gelding two stone better for that run. Second Wind had also won the Herbert Power Handicap at Caulfield just a month back and he was in the stable of Jack Holt, Melbourne's most prolific trainer of winners. Holt had put the polish on such champions as Eurythmic and Heroic.

The odds-on favourite in Second Wind's Herbert Power had been Carradale, the next horse on offer. In the '29 Cup, some observers reckoned that Carradale was travelling as well as anything approaching the corner, but then he dramatically ran off at the home turn. Trainer Jim Scobie wondered if the headstrong colt had headed in that direction because that was where his stable was. Most thought the horse was plain balmy. His owner, LKS Mackinnon, was known to have a bet — in 1914, he had successful wagers of £10,000 to £50, £2000 to £14 and £2000 to £14 about his horse Kingsburgh — but he couldn't be convinced here that Carradale was worth even a pound. The horse did come in for some support, though, most of it from bookmakers who needed to protect themselves after taking some big bets on the Amounis–Carradale double, and he remained on the fourth line of betting.

The announcement of Shadow King's name brought a cheer from the members loyal to their chairman. Clean Sweep and Blue Spec (1905) had won the Moonee Valley Cup before winning the Melbourne Cup, and Stand By in 1924 was a certainty beaten at Flemington after winning at Moonee Valley, so on that basis there was hope. But very few wagers. He finished at 80–1.

In the past 24 hours, Soulton, No. 6, which had run a half-length second to Amounis in the Caulfield Cup, was becoming a lot of people's long shot of choice for the Melbourne Cup. So it was no real surprise when he was backed to win more than £8000 at 20–1. 'Caulfield Cup placegetters often go well in the Melbourne Cup,' Saker's mate advised those around him. To a degree, this was true. While only Poseidon in 1906 had completed the Caulfield Cup-Melbourne Cup double in 52 years, Dunlop (1887), Bravo (1889), Acrasia (1904), Apologue (1907) and Sasanof (1916) had all run second or third at Caulfield before winning at Flemington. Trainer Lou Robertson had sprung a surprise by running Soulton in the Cantala Stakes over a mile on Derby Day, hardly the typical Cup preparation, and the Caulfield Cup second was his only placing this preparation. Then again, he had run third in the 1930 Sydney Cup and would therefore be trying to emulate Windbag and Poitrel, two horses that won the Melbourne Cup after being placed in the Sydney Cup earlier in the year.

Next to be called was Nadean, the hope of South Australia. First call was 33–1, and Harry Lewis jumped on that, taking £3500 to £105, before explaining to the people around him that his jockey had said she was unlucky behind Shadow King in the

Moonee Valley Cup. Optimists recalled the mare's record-breaking win in the Australian Cup at Flemington in the autumn. Realists remembered the way Phar Lap toyed with her when the wonder horse went to Adelaide for the King's Cup two months later. Quickly, two punters connected with the Brodie stable each took a £1000 to £30, and from that moment everyone else had to make do with 28s, then 25s. Out of Mr Lewis' earshot, the consensus was that Nadean would need a fast pace and plenty of luck.

The other South Australian in the field was Some Quality, another mare, a tough but one-paced six-year-old that had finished well back in Nightmarch's Melbourne Cup. A winner of an Australian Cup and a Port Adelaide Cup, and apparently very unlucky when second in the 1927 South Australian Derby, her last three runs had been mediocre. She was sure to get a long way back, probably too far behind, but someone thought she was better than hopeless for she was backed to win £14,000, firming from 100–1 into 66s. That, at this point, was the most money any horse was taking out of the bookies' bags.

Suddenly the building shook, as an explosive burst of thunder shuddered from the night sky. Word flashed through the room that it was absolutely teeming outside, and to say the gale was howling was not doing it justice. What if Flemington turned to mud? Older memories shifted back to 1892, when only 65,000 people braved waterlogged conditions to see the 50–1 outsider, Glenloth, part-owned by a milkman, hurdle a fallen horse before ploughing up the straight to a three-length victory. So thick was the rain and muddy the jockeys' colours at the end of the race, the only way observers could be sure it was Glenloth that had won was the fact that he alone among the Cup field had his tail tied in a knot.

Until the news was leaked a few days earlier that Harry Telford would continue training Phar Lap after his lease ran out, many Sydney racing writers had been suggesting that David Davis' preferred trainer, Chris O'Rourke, would be taking over in the new year. Now, O'Rourke had to make do with trying to get Star God competitive on Cup Day. A number of little bets were made at 100–1, each one followed by a clap of thunder, as if the gods were telling the punters they were wasting their time.

First Acre, the one New Zealand-owned entry, was apparently made of cast iron, having started in nearly 150 races in the past five-and-a-half years. On one visit to Australia he won two races in a single afternoon at Canterbury, but there were plenty of unsuccessful days, too, and his best run in Australia during this preparation was a plugging fifth in the Hotham on Saturday. No one was prepared to bet more than £4 on him, even though there was some 500–1 about. The crowd, it seemed, were much more interested in the three-year-olds.

Ned Moss shifted in his seat as Veilmond's name was called. He was keen to discover who in the room might like his colt's chances. One bookmaker suggested 16–1, then 20s, then 25s — the big punters had clearly seen the way the horse had run up the Flemington straight in the Derby, hanging in on top of Miss Arrow, and concluded he was no genuine stayer. Melbourne Cup winners don't do that sort of thing. Finally, at 50–1, Moss could stand it no more, and he took £1000 to £20, then £2000 to £45. A couple of little bets followed, almost out of sympathy for the owner, it seemed, and then they were all done. Veilmond hadn't been this sort of price since the beginning of August.

As the Cup second favourite, Tregilla had become something of a celebrity, with his supporters keen for any snippet of information they could garner about the chestnut colt. It had been revealed, for example, that — like many other Australian redheads — he was nicknamed 'Bluey'. Before his racing name was called at the Victorian Club, the room was informed that Ted Bartle would be riding three pounds over, at 7.9. The news was greeted with gasps of disbelief. Sure, the Sydney jockey knew the horse, but was he the only accomplished rider available? This was loyalty gone mad — Tregilla's biggest advantage was the huge weight difference between him and Phar Lap, and now they were giving a little bit of it back. 'Do you know only one three-year-old has carried more than 7.9 to win a Melbourne Cup?' Saker's mate had been quiet for a while; now he was astounded. 'Newhaven won with 7.13, but Manfred got beaten with 7.8, Phar Lap with 7.6!'

For all this, the bookmakers seemed hesitant about offering a better price about Tregilla than 7–2, the punters reluctant to accept less than what they could have got on Saturday afternoon. As with Phar Lap, bookies and punters both had their price. A game of bluff was being played, and it wasn't until after the caller said, 'Is that it, gentlemen?', that someone said, '£2250 to £500 is offered.' That was 9–2 and that was close enough to what the punters wanted. Quickly, a trickle became a flood, even though many bookmakers stayed right out of it. Tregilla, in their assessment, was a 7–2 chance and that was where he would stay. In all, more than £3000 was bet, to win around £13,000.

Balloon King had not been compared favourably with Victoria Derby winners of past years, but still he had his admirers and he stayed solid on the third line of betting, at 10–1. Quite quickly, it was time for Muratti. His trainer, Frank Musgrave, had ridden the outsider Goshawk in the Cup in Haricot's year, all of 56 years ago, and trained Vanity Fair into second place behind The Victory in 1902. To the public, Muratti was known as the 'raffle horse', because as a yearling he had been first prize in a draw conducted for charity.

John Wren had then purchased the horse from the owner of the winning ticket, and for a while it seemed he had got himself a really good prospect, though not, it seemed, one that liked winning races. On April Fool's Day, 1929, Muratti finished an unlucky fourth in the Sydney Cup, prompting one Sydney racing scribe to state, 'He can be written down as a horse sure to be in demand for one of the important handicaps of next spring.' The gossip was that after that race, Wren and Musgrave decided to set the horse for the Melbourne Cup, but he broke down and their scheme had to be aborted. Without a win in more than two years, Muratti got into the 1930 Cup with a three-year-old's weight, and until the Hotham he'd shown little form. When Muratti was called, the owner didn't move, but men who it was later revealed were his agents certainly did, and finally this Call of the Card had itself a plunge. By the time it was over, the horse had firmed from 50-1 into 28-1, and bookmakers would be paying out over £20,000 if John Wren finally got to have the starring role at the Melbourne Cup presentation.

The remaining three horses — John Buchan, the three-year-old Wapilly and Jim Scobie's other runner, the Adelaide Cup winner Temptation, came and went with scant interest. Only Malua in 1884 had completed the Adelaide Cup–Melbourne Cup double in the one year, and everyone knew Malua had been a freak horse, winner not just of the Cup but also a six-furlong Newmarket Handicap, an Oakleigh Plate over five-and-a-half furlongs (the start before the two-mile Adelaide Cup!) and a Grand National Hurdle. The rumours were strong that John Buchan was lame and would not start, which helped explain his Hotham failure but also stopped people risking money here.

Wapilly's trainer Mr James Wilson, the son of the founder of St Albans Stud, was happy to tell anyone who'd listen that Tuesday would be the 66th time he was at the Cup, his first-hand memories going right back to Toryboy's win in 1865. Mr Wilson doubted his colt's chances, but was excited to have one more Cup runner of his own, and reacted indignantly when told that a correspondent from the *Sydney Sportsman* had written that Wapilly 'wouldn't win a breadcarters' handicap at Woop Woop'. The Cup memory that gnawed at him most was 1896, the year he found himself the owner/trainer of two highly promising two-year-olds, a filly called Lonely and a colt named Newhaven. He chose to keep Lonely, sold Newhaven for 2000 guineas, and while Lonely never even made it to the racetrack, Newhaven was brilliant in both the Victoria Derby and the Melbourne Cup, his six-length win in the latter race being one of the best ever seen at Flemington.

Three years later came the payback, not just for Mr Wilson but also for Mr Herbert Power, who had been desperately unlucky in 1877 when Chester beat his colt Savanaka. Wilson, as trainer, set Mr Power's three-year-old Merriwee for the Derby–Cup double, and this time the plan worked beautifully. Not even another horribly wet Cup Day could stop them. Before the race, Power told his jockey, 18-year-old Vivian Turner, that Merriwee was a certainty, the 'best horse in the race'. Turner reputedly replied that such were the puddles of water on the Maribyrnong River side he might have to swim around the back of the course.

'Never mind,' Power said with supreme confidence. 'You're on the best swimmer, too.'

Outside the Victorian Club 31 years later, a surprisingly large group of people braved the dreadful conditions to learn if anything sensational had happened at the Call of the Card. Eventually, a club steward came out with a sheet on which he'd written the final prices bet about each horse in the Cup. The market read this way:

Evens	Phar Lap
9–2	Tregilla
10	Balloon King
18	Carradale
20	Soulton
25	Nadean
28	Muratti
35	Veilmond
66	John Buchan, Some Quality, Star God
80	Shadow King, Donald
100	Temptation
125	Second Wind
200	First Acre, Wapilly

As the rain eased for a moment, but the strong wind continued to blow, a bevy of club patrons ducked out, past the punters passing the sheet of paper around, heading off into the night. Saker was among them, but while he was going home to sleep, most others were hoping to reach their next engagement reasonably dry and with umbrella intact. Fat chance of that; soon the rain was dumping down once more. The prospect was a heavy track. Could it be that Phar Lap, like Merriwee, would need to be not only the best horse in the Melbourne Cup, but the best swimmer, too?

CHAPTER THIRTEEN

UNDER ATTACK

WOODCOCK HAD NEVER SEEN weather like this. First it was the fine dust, which smothered the sky to such an extent that dusk came four hours early. Then came the distant thunder and the mass of lightning, which shimmered atop the north-western horizon like a faulty light bulb. Then the copper-coloured rain that poured through the sky, quickly forming puddles — no, rivers — of water that cut through the stud's paths and tracks and made the area between the stables and the imposing St Albans homestead a treacherous sea of mud. After that there was the wind, for a little while like a cyclone and then a constant, throbbing gale that tore at the trees and roofs and roughly threw buckets, boxes, fossils and firewood to all points of the property. Inside Phar Lap's stall, Woodcock and Parker tried valiantly and to a degree successfully to calm their friend, while never quite being sure that the end of the world wasn't near. An impossibly angry crack of thunder, surely only feet away, shook the entire district and a block of wood, maybe a fence post that must've been flying horizontally, crashed into the side of the stable. Then there was a bang at the stable door, and a drenched Guy Raymond dashed in to make sure everything was all right.

'Gee, Mr Raymond, you're putting on quite a show,' Woodcock laughed weakly.

'Are you all okay in here?' Raymond asked.

'I think it'll be all right,' said Woodcock. 'This is one mighty fine building.'

Indeed it was. They all owed a debt of gratitude to James Wilson senior, who had not spared a penny in building St Albans into one of Australia's finest properties of the 19th century. Woodcock, Parker and Phar Lap also owed much to Raymond and Hugh Ranken, who had so dutifully set about returning the stud to the standards of its heyday.

'At least the rain'll keep the crooks away,' Parker remarked dryly. It was the first time Raymond had heard the young apprentice talk.

'Do not be so sure,' the old army captain responded quickly. 'If they are about, the storm won't stop them. It will be cover for them. We must be vigilant. You men stay in here. I will keep guard outside.'

No sooner had these words passed Raymond's lips and there was a flash of lightning, another enormous burst of thunder, and then a second lightning shot so vivid that for a moment it lit the interior of the stable on its own. Perhaps it had struck a tree outside, or even the homestead? Raymond dashed outside to check for damage but was just as quickly back, water dripping from his hat, his raincoat freshly awash. However, before he could offer any reassurance there was another violent flash of lightning, and then it was pitch black. The lights were gone. Had the power failed? Or were they under attack?

'I'll call Constable Hazel,' Raymond said loudly, battling to make himself heard above the pounding of the rain on the roof, as he searched for the kerosene lamps he had shrewdly left on a bench. Hazel, he knew, was one of the policemen on duty at Geelong — the St Albans owner had contacted the station during the day, just in case, to confirm that their roster for the next 24 hours had not been changed, and to determine again precisely who was the right man to call in an emergency. John Hazel was also an AIF man, rising to the rank of Sergeant-Major during the War, which was so much the better. The phone, of course, was in the homestead, so the stud owner had to briefly leave Woodcock and Parker with Phar Lap; when he did, all the two young men could do was see in each other's face the alarm each was now feeling.

Within a minute, Raymond was back. The phone line was dead, he couldn't get through. But as they began to comprehend what this might mean, Mrs Raymond — inevitably saturated, poor woman — was knocking on the stable door to say that she'd found a line. Raymond went back to the homestead with her, but as he did so another terrifying thunderclap rent the air, shaking a lamp off its perch near the window and making Woodcock instinctively grab too tight on Phar Lap's bridle. His terror was translated to his horse, who for the first time during the storm really began to show his displeasure, jumping back and throwing his head about. Woodcock could only purr at him and keep his face reassuringly close, while Parker warily patted Phar Lap's rump and tried to sound calm as he whispered, 'Whoa, Bobby, whoa boy.'

Again Raymond was back quickly, and again the news was bad. The line was definitely dead. The power in the house was gone, too. It could have been the lightning, fallen power poles, blown fuses, all sorts of calamities were possible in these conditions. Who knows what might have happened to the telephone exchange? But they also had to accept the possibility that it might be foul play. 'Men, we have to assume the worst,' Raymond ordered. 'If there are people out there who want to do us harm, we are dreadfully outnumbered. I will have to go into Geelong myself and fetch Constable Hazel. It is not worth the risk to sit here and believe we can handle this ourselves.'

It was five miles into the centre of town. In this weather, that was at least 15 minutes each way, plus however much time Raymond needed at the station to convince Hazel and Hazel's superiors that St Albans Stud was where the constable had to be. As he drove as fast as he dared through this awful night, maybe 25 miles an hour, his eyes straining to make out the road through the gloom, the shame of 'losing' Phar Lap consumed him. That could not happen. At least no one else was crazy enough to be on the road in this weather, and he was explaining his situation to Hazel quicker than he could have hoped.

'Phar Lap!' exclaimed the constable, who was maybe 40 years old, fair-skinned, not too tall and carrying a few pounds. 'At St Albans? I did not know.'

'I am sure your sergeant is aware,' Raymond replied anxiously. 'Is he here?'

'Sergeant Baker,' Hazel called out, 'Mr Raymond from St Albans would like to see you.'

Baker was at the counter in an instant. 'Is everything all right, Mr Raymond?' he said.

'Our power is out, the phone is dead, we are defenceless at the moment,' Raymond snapped as politely as he could. 'I presume the police in Melbourne have told you about Phar Lap?'

'Yes, Jack Brophy contacted me on Saturday night,' Baker said, 'told me the horse was coming here. Asked me to inform as few people as possible. I took that to mean, "Tell no one."'

'Is there any way Constable Hazel can come with me tonight? I fear there might be trouble.'

'Gee, Mr Raymond, we've got damage everywhere. It's not just you who's lost power. There's telegraph poles down in South and East Geelong. The phones across the city got knocked out at seven o'clock. Live wires down in a couple of places, the hospital is blacked out. Roofs been blown away, the trains are out. But it is the Cup favourite. I suppose you can take Hazel for now, but if things get worse, I'll have to come and get him.'

'Thank you, Sergeant,' Raymond responded. 'I'll try to bring him back in one piece.'

The two men walked outside into the storm. 'Hazel, I am going up to Aberdeen Street, to get some more help. Can you drive straight to St Albans? Tommy Woodcock is the name of the lad looking after Phar Lap. I will meet you there.'

FROM NOT LONG AFTER Mr Raymond left, Woodcock, Parker and Phar Lap were down to one kerosene lamp. The gale grew worse, to the point where they were sure it was going to clean lift the stable off its foundations, and though the thunder and lightning had dissipated, it was as if they were no longer necessary, as if they'd been the cannon fire that'd paved the way for the infantry. Phar Lap was as edgy as he'd ever been, in an environment he didn't know, hearing noises and feeling vibrations that were totally foreign to him. In his eyes was something Woodcock had never seen in his friend before: fear. What might this do to his Cup tomorrow? And then it happened — the stable door burst open, almost off its hinges, and Woodcock spun around expecting to see a platoon of armed gunmen flooding through the door. Instead, there were branches, leaves, mud and rain exploding in, and Parker sprinted out into the storm, grabbed the door handle with strength he never knew and pulled it back shut. Then he pushed a table hard up against the door, illogical given that it opened out, and lifted a couple of timber boxes full of tools and junk up onto the table. He checked the latch, and turned the key so hard it had to be locked tight. No way was that door getting opened until Mr Raymond got back.

But why was he taking so long? The rain eased, but in many ways that was worse because instead of the constant hammer of water on roof, now the sounds outside were indiscriminate. When a branch crackled, was it being blown away or trodden on? A quick look through the window revealed shadows everywhere, none of them familiar. Then, finally, a car pulled up; horribly, it was one Woodcock did not know. A fat man got out, and stood there, waiting, it seemed, for another vehicle that was following. Woodcock looked at the bloke standing by that first car and chillingly saw that he was wearing a cap, a motor driver's cap, like you see in the movies. It was the same cap that the bloke had been wearing in Manchester Grove on Derby Day. 'Jeez, Bobby, kill the light,' Woodcock cried at Parker. 'Get your head down, I think this is it.'

Parker had the lamp off in a moment. No one moved. When Phar Lap snorted it sounded like a firecracker had gone off. As often as he dared, Woodcock snuck another peek out the window, but the intruder outside stayed by his car, cap on, collar up, looking back at the stud entrance as though he was expecting others. In his right hand, no doubt about it, was a rifle. Where was Mr Raymond? Christ, I hope he's all right. He looked again at the cap the man was wearing. It was definitely the same one ...

Or was it? Hang on, that's a police constable's cap! And that second car just arriving ... that's Mr Raymond. 'It's all right, don't worry,' Woodcock said sheepishly. 'You'd better get that table away from the door.'

Unfortunately, Bobby Parker was all but frozen by terror. He was able to meekly push at the table and release the lock, but he couldn't move the door, not right now. Raymond had to pull it open, and when he saw the shellshocked look on the apprentice's colourless, callow face, his immediate reaction was to dread what might be further inside. 'Hold on, son, I will be with you in a moment,' he said kindly, his hand on Parker's shoulder. Woodcock was busy with Phar Lap, rubbing the champion's neck, wiping the sweat from his stomach and between his hind legs. 'It nearly got a bit much for us, Mr Raymond,' the strapper said, reassuringly calm now. 'We was seeing and hearing things that weren't there.'

Constable Hazel was introduced, as was Norman Belcher, another of Raymond's AIF colleagues, who'd jumped at the call-up when Raymond knocked on his door. Belcher was a Gallipoli veteran, part of the 1st Light Horse, and a member of one of Geelong's most respected families, having been born down at Leopold, a few miles east of St Albans, in 1879, Darriwell's year. Despite the reinforcements, Parker refused an offer to go over to the homestead. 'I'm all right,' he said weakly, but defiantly, 'I want to stay with Tommy and the horse.'

As if to confirm the worst had passed, at that very moment the lights flickered back to life. Raymond went through his plan: that he, Belcher and Hazel would be outside, while Woodcock and Parker remained inside the stable with Phar Lap. If either of the lads wanted a rest in the house, they were most welcome. The rain was easing now, and the wind would exhaust itself around midnight. Before that, around half-past nine, the power would go again, but by then the only way of realising that had happened was that Mrs Raymond's reading lamp near the window across from the stable suddenly died. She had said she was going to stay up as late as she could, to bring more cups of tea and offer support any way she could. Meanwhile, had Hazel been realistic about his situation, he might have concluded that there were much more essential services for a constable in Geelong to be providing on this wretched night than being at St Albans, especially since Belcher was also on guard.

He never did. He was protecting Phar Lap the night before the Melbourne Cup. It was cold now, the temperatures having dropped appreciably since the storm passed through, and the rain continued to fall, though more a drizzle than torrential. He was standing ankle-deep in mud, and though he liked Mr Raymond and loved the ambience and stately manner of St Albans Stud, he was growing tired of being told that you can never be too careful. He wondered, if for no other reason than the appalling weather, whether the likelihood of an attack was almost zero. However, he'd read about the shooting and that the gangsters would stop at nothing, so soon he was picturing the various ways the villains could strike. This was real police work. There was no place he would rather be.

CHAPTER FOURTEEN

THE CASE IS CLOSED

IF PARKER SLEPT AT all during the night, it did him no good. Woodcock didn't even try. Before the rooster crowed, the two were out talking with Raymond while Belcher and Hazel stayed alert, making plans to give Phar Lap the gallop they knew he needed. This was something the strapper and the stud owner had discussed the previous afternoon, and not long after 5am the Cup favourite was loaded onto St Albans' small float for the short drive to Geelong racecourse. They could have walked, but why take the risk? When they arrived, Raymond guided them not through the front entrance, but down to the back of the course, to a rarely used gate. Once through that, he and Hazel removed a section of the outside rail to let Parker aboard Phar Lap and Woodcock on one of St Albans' horses, Sledmere Bill, go three furlongs together in good style. Raymond was stunned. He knew as well as anyone that Phar Lap was a champion, but after everything they'd been through in the past few hours and over the past three days, surely the horse was entitled to be off his game.

Instead, it was as if the change of surroundings had done him good. He was bright and his coat was shiny and immaculate. He was back at the stud before seven, seemingly oblivious to the exhaustion around him, and later that morning Woodcock even took him for another short walk, just to make sure he wasn't too relaxed. Telford, Boyden and the police weren't due until half eleven, and the three or four hours before that were always going to be long ones. Raymond and Belcher kept their field glasses and rifles close at hand, while Hazel agreed to stay until Phar Lap and his entourage were on their way to Flemington. His shift was over, but in his mind the job was not.

BACK IN MELBOURNE, the city was mopping up after the carnage of the previous evening. The stories of damage from across Victoria were astonishing. In the *Age* a column was devoted to tales of how the dust, wind and rain had cut through the towns of the western half of the state: 'Darkness at Mildura', 'Storm at Nhill', 'Damage at Horsham', 'Electric Light Fails at Echuca', 'Rough Day at Ballarat', 'Havoc at Warrnambool', 'Lights out in Geelong', the paragraphs ran one after the other. In the city itself, the Harrison Stand at the Melbourne Cricket Ground had seen its iron roof blown into a nearby park and the ground's big scoreboard had also been damaged. Several large trees had been uprooted in Fitzroy Gardens. At Port Melbourne, where the navy ship *Canberra* had just arrived so its sailors could see the Cup, the officer on watch spotted a hefty object half submerged being blown across Port Phillip Bay and assumed it was a stray boat. Actually, it was a raft, weighing more than a ton, which was being used for reconstruction work at Princes Pier before it took off into the night. Power poles were down in many Melbourne suburbs, live wires remained a threat to motorists and pedestrians, plate-glass windows had blown out, tree branches were strewn across the streets.

At Flemington, the gardens were a badly beaten shadow of their Derby Day glory. The roses near the judge's box were shredded. Lines of banksias had been ripped asunder, while beds of poppies, ranunculus and nemesia had seen their brilliance shattered in the space of a few wet and windswept hours. Equally as bedraggled were the tiers of monkey musk, pansies and violas, so beautiful on the Saturday that crowds had gathered to admire the horticulturists' work. The large elms were now painted with dollops of red mud, while the green lawns still looked pretty from a distance but were treacherous to walk on. Only around the Members Stand, where the palms and ferns had been sheltered from the full fury of the storm, was the beauty intact. And, of course, things were also grand in the vice-regal suite and the Governor's Room, where the table decorations, featuring pink roses, carnations, water lilies, trails of asparagus fern, soft blue violas and butterfly delphiniums were going to be splendid.

The *Canberra* was not the only notable visitor to Port Melbourne. Other ships now berthed there included the impressive RMS *Oronsay*, which had brought not only the Australian cricketers to Melbourne but also Cup devotees from Perth and Adelaide, and the *Katoomba*, which had departed Sydney on the Saturday with 300 people on board, among them Mrs Maude Vandenburg, who'd spent part of her Caulfield Cup winnings on a first-class ticket. While the total number of visitors in Melbourne was down on the pre-depression days, lots of men, women and children from interstate had arrived by boat, car, train and even plane, sometimes paying for tickets with money they did not have, in the hope that a few shrewd or lucky bets might save the day. Those who'd driven in from Sydney told of the vagabonds walking sadly but determinedly on the side of the road, the soles of their shoes long worn through, in the process of transferring their sorry existences to Melbourne. With nothing more to lose, they'd timed their migration to coincide with the Cup.

At Russell Street, Brophy and Saker were scouring the papers, searching for references to the Phar Lap shooting. There was next to nothing. The *Age* did manage to mention the 'recent sensational happenings at Caulfield' in one report, but only as a means of explaining the large crowd that gathered there on the Monday to see Old Ming gallop. The *Sun News-Pictorial* and the *Argus* were similar. The case was closed. However, policemen still needed to be sent out to Geelong to give Telford and his horse an escort to the Cup, because to not do so would raise questions they didn't want the outside world to ask. And what if copycats or genuine hoodlums now tried to do what the press boys couldn't? So, as had been arranged, four officers — two on motorcycles and two to ride in the float with Woodcock, Boyden, Telford and Phar Lap — were despatched to St Albans. Brophy and Saker would meet the favourite when he arrived at the track.

Cup Day trains and trams to Flemington commenced at 9am, with services reaching a peak at noon, when a train or tram would be arriving at Flemington just about every other minute. While most roads led to the track on this public holiday throughout Victoria, not all did, with special services also departing for Melbourne's beaches, and to bush towns on the fringe of the city such as Hurstbridge, Warbuton and Fern Tree Gully. As many as 20,000 people were expected to descend on Wattle Park, east of the city centre, where 25 separate 'Sunday School picnics' were to be held. As the day moved on, it would become clear that the official attendance at Flemington would be down on previous years, as would the patronage of these public transport services. This was attributed in part to the weather, and also to the exorbitant fares charged — you needed to spend three shillings to catch a return train from Flinders Street station in the city to the racetrack platform situated adjacent to the course. By lunchtime, more than 4000 cars would be parked in the official racecourse carpark, which led some to comment that there had to be something wrong if so many people preferred to fight the traffic than use the trains. The days when horse-drawn 'drags' would deliver their passengers to the course were all but gone; there were a few among the line of traffic that edged from the city to the track, but not many.

STAN BOYDEN FIRED THE engine of his float at precisely 10.30am. The previous afternoon, he'd rendezvoused with Harry Telford in the city in somewhat bizarre circumstances. Having been told to be outside a small saddlery business on Bourke Street at a particular time, Boyden saw Telford walk towards him, collar of his jacket pulled high, the brim of his hat tugged low, his nose pointing at the footpath. Phar Lap's trainer was clearly nervous, and like an actor in a low-budget movie he looked up and down the street before muttering instructions. 'Tomorrow morning at 11, 10 miles out of the city, on the Geelong Road, you'll see a police car parked,' he whispered. 'I'll be in it. You pull over, and I'll travel with you to St Albans.'

And there they were. Boyden parked his vehicle and immediately Phar Lap's trainer jumped in the passenger seat. There was no warm greeting, just a 'You might need this' as he handed him a revolver.

'Careful, it's loaded,' Telford muttered.

Boyden didn't offer a word. He looked at Telford and the police outside, slipped the gun in his pocket and assumed that the trainer had one of his own that he'd use if necessary. The engine was still running — a little roughly, it must be said — a motorcyclist took off, the float slipped in behind him, then the second bike followed, with a police car at the rear. About the only thing Telford said for the rest of the trip came when he explained that the motor trailing them was a 'wireless patrol car' so they could contact Melbourne if anything happened. Boyden was past thinking about whether something was ever going to go wrong, but he couldn't help pondering how many police vehicles were set up with two-way wirelesses. It couldn't have been many.

It had rained off and on all morning, and shortly before they got into Geelong it really poured. This meant that very few people saw the convoy rumble through town, but enough, and word shot around the shops and streets that 'right here' might be where Phar Lap had been hiding. At St Albans, the loading of the rugged-up gelding onto the float was completed with military precision. Bang on noon, Telford barked, 'Righto, Stan, let's get going.' Boyden wound up the crank handle, and the motor gave barely a chug. 'Come on, man, we haven't got all day!' He tried again and again there was little sign of life. The stunned silence was palpable. In deliberately keeping it as late as possible to get to the track, Telford had left no room for error. 'Here, let me have a go,' said one of the constables. Nothing. A third policeman tried his darnedest, as Boyden stared at his waterlogged engine. Woodcock stayed with his horse, who was growing restless, stuck in his cramped surroundings while the men swore and swapped roles outside. Of all the long half hours of these four days in November, this was the longest. Finally, there was a spark, and the engine spluttered, ticked over, coughed again, and then rumbled into something that resembled life.

Telford ran over to Raymond and the two shook hands, exchanged gazes for a moment, and then grabbed each other in a bear hug. What the owner of this great stud had done for him was not something the former battler would forget. It had restored some of his faith in humanity.

'I hope he wins the race for you,' Raymond said. 'I am sure he will.'

'He certainly looks well enough. You've done a wonderful thing for me,' Telford replied.

'It was not me, Harry. That Woodcock is quite a horseman. Both your lads are excellent. But enough of this, you must be on your way. I will see you at the track.'

So, as quickly as Boyden dared, they were on their way, back through town, onto the highway to Melbourne, to the Cup. Down the main street of Geelong, many stopped to stare, point and wave at the mini-motorcade, and old-timers reminisced about the days when James Wilson senior used to set off with his team for the Cup and the locals would come out to cheer them on their way. Woodcock, Parker and a policeman rode with Phar Lap in the float, with Telford and another policeman alongside Boyden up front, and the bikes and car leading and trailing as before. Of course, the police escort meant that the float received a saloon passage for the entire journey, which might have been lucky. Had the ailing Brockway been caught in traffic, the lengthy hold-up might have killed the engine stone dead.

CHAPTER FIFTEEN

CUP DAY

IT WAS THE GREAT American writer Samuel Langhorne Clemens, better known as Mark Twain, who, after experiencing Auraria's Cup of 1895, described Flemington as 'the Mecca of Australia'. Few overseas visitors have been more taken by the event than Twain, who in his book *Following the Equator* (published in 1897) suggested that ...

> Cup Day, and Cup Day only, commands an attention, an interest, and an enthusiasm which are universal — and spontaneous, not perfunctory. Cup Day is supreme, it has no rival. I can call to mind no specialized annual day, in any country, which can be named by that large name — Supreme. I can call to mind no specialized annual day, in any country, whose approach fires the whole land with a conflagration of conversation and preparation and anticipation and jubilation. No day save this one; but this one does it ...

In 1895, Melbourne was a city of half a million people, having had a bigger population than Sydney for 35 years since the phenomenal gold boom of the 1850s changed the Australian landscape. Through the 1870s and '80s, the city had continued to quickly expand, largely on the back of much uncontrolled speculation in urban land, but things went awry in the 1890s, to the point that when Twain visited the city its citizens were in the middle of a harsh economic downturn. So it was not just in terms of the extraordinary national interest in the race that the Cup pageant of 1930 mirrored that of 1895. Carbine's Cup of 1890 had been worth an astonishing £13,230 (including a trophy valued at £150), with £10,080 and the cup going to Mr Donald Wallace, the winning owner. But underlining the extent of the plight that soon overtook the nation, five years later the total purse had declined to £3667. It wasn't until 1921 that prizemoney climbed back above £10,000. The richest of the first 69 Cups was 1923, when Bitalli and company raced for £13,488 (including a trophy valued at £200). The field in 1930 would be competing for £12,429, with £9229 and a £200 cup going to the owners of the first horse across the line, £2000 to second and £1000 to third.

Across Australia, people young and old were relying on the wireless, a technology that had really only taken hold in the past five years, to bring them a description of the great race. In the bush, some were stopping work and travelling vast distances to be near a race call when the field jumped away. Later, many would head to the cinema to see black-and-white footage of the Cup via the 'talkie' newsreel produced by Australian Movietone News. Newspapers across the country had provided extensive Cup previews and were already planning their post-Cup editions, while a significant number of punters from all parts had the

Amounis–Phar Lap double running and a fortunate few had live tickets in one of the big 'Tatt's' sweepstakes.

One person in line for a big payout from Tatt's was Constable Archie Campbell of nearby Footscray, who was part of a syndicate that also included his wife, other family members and two men who had been unemployed for months. They would win £15,000 if Phar Lap prevailed. A little less than 2000 miles away, Alick Homewood, once a good amateur jockey, now getting by at Hughenden in far north Queensland, had Phar Lap in another big draw. 'Sweeps' had become a constant of the Cup, whether they be small office or family affairs, where everyone put maybe a sixpence in and drew a horse from a hat, or massive enterprises such as those conducted by the big lotteries agent, Tattersall's (hence Tatt's), a venture initiated by an adventurous Sydney publican named George Adams back in the 1880s. In these much publicised draws, tens of thousands of tickets were sold, some lucky punters had horses in the final field, and extremely nervous souls such as Constable Campbell and Mr Homewood found themselves with the Cup favourite at life-changing odds.

THE MEMBERS' PRIVATE RESERVE at Flemington was dominated by a three-level grandstand that was constructed through 1922 and 1923, and looked out over the lawn onto the track from the furlong pole to the half-furlong. Ground level contained the stewards' room, the weigh-in area, office space and a big luncheon room. The first floor contained another dining facility and the vice-regal suite, both of which opened out into an area from where the race could be observed. The top deck provided seating for 6500 spectators, more than half reserved exclusively for members. Alternatively, races could be watched from the lawn in front of the stand. Apart from the members, also invited into the

Members Reserve this day were the connections of the Cup horses, including, of course, David Davis and his wife, the Victorian members of the Australian cricket team, Lord Somers, the acting Governor-General, and Lady Somers, Victoria's Lieutenant-Governor, Sir William Irvine, and Lady Irvine, South Australia's Governor, Sir Alexander Hore-Ruthven, and Lady Hore-Ruthven, and Sir Otto Niemeyer, a senior Treasury official from London who had been sent to Australia to report on the ailing economy. Later in the day, the Somers were joined by their daughter, The Hon. Elizabeth Somers Cocks, who was wearing a fawn tweed belted coat and a soft felt hat in a slightly paler shade, just one of a welter of fashions to be reported in fine detail in the women's section of Wednesday's papers.

The VRC split their licensed bookmakers into three categories: 'Paddock', 'Hill' and 'Flat', the Paddock bookies being the elite. The prime positions in the main betting ring were reserved for the boldest of the bagmen and were located along the barrier, or 'rail', that separated the members from the public. The 'rails' bookmakers could thus accept bets from punters in both the members and the general admission areas. In the hour before any big race, the bookies' rings could be fascinating places, as punters watched and listened intently, in case a plunge was instigated or a horse started 'blowing' dramatically from short to much longer odds. Horses that 'eased' from, say, 4–1 to 10s rarely won, and the seasoned observers knew it. Conversely, if a horse starting 'firming' from 10–1 to fours many of the punters were rapidly elbowing their way towards the bookmakers. Experienced horse players had their preferred places from where they could observe the fluctuations, and they could be incredibly polite so long as they weren't distracted. But then they'd see a plunge coming or discover half a point over the price they wanted and it was every man for himself.

In 1895, the favourite started at 5–1. Half an hour before race one, the Cup hurdle, 35 years later, Bob Jansen called out, '5 to 4 Phar Lap' and immediately Sam Sullivan claimed him for £5000 to £4000. The wager was accepted without emotion, but when straight afterwards another man sought a mere £500 to £400, Jansen said, 'No, I'm sorry, sir, he's evens now.'

'Thanks, Bob, I appreciate it,' Sullivan said after the disappointed punter stormed off.

'It's okay, cobber,' Jansen replied. 'I hope the money stays in my bag.'

'So do I, mate, so do I.'

Overnight, Sullivan had done his sums one last time. Retrieving 5000 quid if Phar Lap won wouldn't solve his problems, but it would help a little. Trouble was, having handed £4000 over to the leader of the ring, now he'd be a loser if just about anything won. But he wouldn't be out of business unless Phar Lap prevailed. Ideally, he told Jansen, he needed something like John Buchan or Wapilly to come through for him. And then he heard someone say, 'There's two horses been scratched from the Cup.' Sullivan knew which two. Wapilly had come out as 12.06pm, John Buchan at 12.25.

'Do you know, a bloke came up to me just a minute back and asked what price Phar Lap not running?' Jansen told him.

'Jeez, I hadn't heard that one,' Sullivan replied, thinking immediately that he might have just thrown away four grand. The whole idea behind waiting as late as possible to lay off some of his Phar Lap debts had been the hope that maybe he wouldn't start. 'I did hear them on the wireless this morning wondering where he is. Can you imagine the hullabaloo if they still haven't found him when they jump!'

'No, I think it'll be all right,' Jansen said quietly. 'The club had

Telford in here yesterday afternoon. I'm sure they know what's going on.'

Telford had indeed been invited to meet with the VRC Secretary Arthur Kewney, and had come to the club's offices not long after he met Boyden in the city. Afterwards, there was confirmation to reporters that the meeting took place, but little else. Privately, Kewney was most annoyed that he hadn't been told where the Cup favourite was staying. Didn't the damn man trust him?

'The shooting is purely a matter between Mr Telford and the police,' Kewney stated for the public record. 'Had it occurred on Flemington racecourse, it would have been a matter for the club.'

RIGHT NOW, WHAT WAS a serious concern for the VRC was the weather, which was taxing the racecourse infrastructure to the limit and making the track itself more and more rain-affected. Shortly after noon, a terrific hailstorm blanketed Flemington; it wasn't the first time it had rained during the day, just easily the worst. However, after it passed, the masses cheerfully poured once more back to their sodden vantage points and resumed their conversations and picnics as if nothing had happened. While the members' lawn was not as congested as in previous years, that vast wonderful viewing area known as the 'Hill' seemed as tightly jammed as ever. As the Cup drew closer, and all viable vantage points disappeared, late arrivals from the betting ring and a few other brave individuals took to the most slippery parts, clinging to fence poles to maintain balance, but sometimes losing their grip and sliding into their brethren below. Alternatively, patrons could go down to the lawn around the saddling paddock at the eastern end of the big grandstand or into the top deck of the stand, but of course they had to pay extra for such privileges.

Even on an afternoon when it was exposed and chilly, the Hill was the most popular place on Cup Day. As many as 50,000 people could get a good view of the race by packing into this part of the course. Practically everyone in 1930 had a hat, most men with ties, the ladies wearing frocks that dropped as far as or just above the ankle. The terrain the Hill covered extended up and back from the track to the northerly and western boundaries of the course, starting before the winning post, adjacent to the Members Stand, and wrapping right around to where the old, more open birdcage used to be located, beyond the turn out of the main straight, down near the Maribyrnong River. It was a huge natural viewing area, with a covered terrace cut into the beginning of the upslope, and then another covered section right at the back. The Hill offered panoramic views of the entire course, even if the people on the Flat, on the infield of the course, looked like a distant army, and those scouting for a free view over on 'Scotchman's Hill', on the far side of the river, in the suburb of Footscray, seemed smaller still.

The record official attendance for a Cup was the 118,877 who saw Spearfelt triumph in 1926; some reckoned the crowd inside the course in 1930 was only three-quarters of that. It was certainly apparent that the attendance on the Flat was significantly down on past Cups. This left plenty of room for the kids to play and smaller queues than usual for them to wait to jump on the merry-go-round or enjoy the pony rides, but there were still too many people for the few covered areas, so almost everyone was soaked to the skin after the tempest struck at midday. Vans and tents offering food and beer were as prevalent as always, and there were plenty of bookmakers and makeshift totes to contend with, though some operations were clearly not as trustworthy as they could have been. The patrons here were not as well dressed as those on the other side of the track, and in the case of an unkempt few it appeared that their suits and shoes had been purchased in less stressful times. Much more prominent on the Flat were punters from foreign shores — Chinese, Indian and European — who seemed content to emerge from their own tight blocs only to spar with the bookies.

As on the Hill, there were plenty of family picnics and many one-shilling and two-shilling bets to be made on the Flat, and no shortage of advice for the jockeys as they made their way to the start for the three races — the hurdle, a six-furlong highweight handicap and a two-year-old sprint — that preceded the main event. In each case, the most athletic among the Flat patrons would try to follow the race by running from one part of the inside rail to another, creating an impression for those on the Hill of ants running in all directions as the horses made their way from start to finish. Most, though, would congregate near the winning post and rely on the rumbling cheers from the flashier viewing areas to tell them the horses were fast approaching.

Among the spectators on the Flat was Mr William Henderson, a former mayor of Williamstown, who was attending his 65th Melbourne Cup. His Cup memories went right back to Banker's win in 1863. 'In those days there weren't public conveyances such as there are today,' he explained to a reporter from the Herald. 'Most people walked. I always took a position at the entrance to the home straight, where you can see which horse is going to win.'

Mr Henderson remembered with a smile The Assyrian's year, 1882, when thousands left Flemington immediately after the race because there was nowhere to stand — the torrential rain that fell throughout the afternoon had turned the Flat into a lake! So brutal was Melbourne's weather that first Tuesday in November, the jockeys went to the start wearing overcoats.

'Why, sir, are you here on the Flat and not in the stands?' asked the journalist.

'I have always been a patron of the Flat,' Mr Henderson replied respectfully, as if he was talking about being a member of a prestigious club. 'I've never bet more than 10 shillings in my life, and I'd be here even if I didn't have a penny on.'

A sense of community also existed up on Scotchman's Hill, which was located about half a mile from the winning post and gave those unable or unwilling to pay for admission to the track a reasonably clear, if often distant, view of the happenings on course. Never had this elevated piece of parkland been more popular for a Cup than on this occasion. The surrounding streets were teeming with cars and pedestrians, and from 10.30am the crowds around the park's entrance gates were as large and animated as if a big game of cricket or football was to be staged inside. Perhaps 40,000 people gathered here, many to try to watch the race, others just to savour the occasion. A silver coin collection was made for the unemployed. There were rascals about, too, keen to swindle unsuspecting individuals they considered fair game, and unscrupulous, unregistered bookies with similar if more sophisticated plans. However, there were also a number of people happy to inhibit such schemes, so the attempts at skulduggery could offer entertainment value of their own.

A second, smaller group of racegoers sat on a mound to the east of the track, near the abattoirs, a long, long way from the action. But as on Scotchman's Hill, the price of admission was perfect and the mood right for a holiday.

DESPITE THE CONTRASTING SOCIAL climes from where the people came, one topic of conversation eclipsed all others: where was Phar Lap? This was true across Australia, as Cup Day lunches were in full swing, office parties began, jackaroos rode into stations, SPs set up in public bars, farmers called it a day, lawyers sought adjournments, wireless salesmen prepared for an avalanche of 'customers' keen to experience their finest product, teachers and students made plans for quick getaways the moment the bell went ...

Around Flemington racecourse, only four men knew for sure where the gelding had been: Detectives Brophy and Saker, Commissioner Blamey and David Davis. Jim Pike sat in the far corner of the jockey's room, smoking yet another cigarette and getting more and more sick and tired of people not believing him when he said he did not know. In the VRC Committee room and among the vice-regal guests, however, many now had a fair idea, after a call was received from Mr Guy Raymond from St Albans, apologising for not being able to make it to lunch and asking if special arrangements could be made for when Phar Lap, Telford and their police escort arrived at the course. Perhaps the back entrance to the course, away from the public milling near the front gate, could be manned rather than locked as it usually was on race days?

Mr Raymond, eh? So that's where the champion has been. Then reports from Geelong began to come through, saying that the horse and his minders had been spotted driving through town a little after 12.30pm, confirming the St Albans connection beyond doubt. Unless the traffic was bad, or something went terribly wrong, Phar Lap would be at Flemington by around two o'clock. The Cup was set to go at 3.30pm.

So how come it was now nearly quarter past two, and there was still no sign of him?

CHAPTER SIXTEEN

PRIDE, RAGE AND DREAD

'ARE YOU SURE YOU'RE on our side?' Telford looked at Boyden with a mixture of anger and exasperation etched across his face. It was the third time the float driver had pulled over, fearful his engine was going to die completely. No way would he have dared turning the motor off — that might have been the end. How ridiculous would they all look if a miserable old Brockway truck was able to do what the gangsters couldn't: stop Phar Lap from running in the Cup.

'I'll get you there, Mr Telford,' was Boyden's tired response. He grabbed the grimy towel he was using to dry the motor and did whatever it was that had to be done as quickly as he could, and then the journey was resumed, all the while the engine answering back whenever he dared to accelerate too hard.

It probably wasn't until they got about a mile from the course, with the grandstand in sight, that Telford was able to rule out 'float broke down' as the reason he missed the Cup. He reckoned they could walk the rest of the way and Phar Lap would arrive in time to make it to the start. 'What's the latest time before the race you can actually get there?' the policeman with them asked, to which Telford grumbled an inaudible reply that the officer took to mean either 'Don't know' or 'None of your business'. If Phar Lap was 20–1 in an inconsequential handicap on a Saturday in the middle of winter and he hadn't turned up an hour-and-a-half before the race, the stewards might have scratched him. Different race, different horse.

They landed at Flemington about 2.25pm. There was barely enough time to get him to the birdcage, where they were met by Brophy, Saker and, inevitably, a battalion of plain-clothes officers, ready to stand guard. 'You'll be all right, Harry,' Brophy said quietly. 'No one will be game to have a pop at him now.' There was no right time or reason to explain that the shooting had been a stunt, and there never would be. Just 15 minutes after the champion arrived in his stall, Woodcock was reaching for the saddle to get him ready for the race. A blacksmith whisked off Phar Lap's shoes and replaced them with racing plates. The crowd that had been milling around the stalls all afternoon suddenly converged on the favourite's stall, No. 53, after the word buzzed around the course that he was finally here.

'Where is he?' a woman asked, to be quickly directed to the far end, where the punters were shoulder to shoulder. Some horses in nearby stalls grew restless with the hubbub around them, but Phar Lap was unflappable, a reporter who identified himself as being from the *Age* remarking that the gelding didn't look so much unconcerned as bored.

'Carbine was quiet like that,' one sage in the crowd responded.

'So was Poseidon,' stated another. 'All great horses are the same.'

A young lady, frustrated at not being able to get so much as a peek at her hero, cried out, 'You would think he was the only horse in the race!'

'So he is!' a devoted male fan asserted.

The bookmakers were rock solid in this view. Hard as they tried, they couldn't find enough support for Tregilla to bring his price in from 9–2. Instead, he drifted out to fives. Phar Lap went from evens to 10–9 on, 5–4 on, 11–8 on. It was mostly little people's money, as if all the once-a-year punters had decided that the Cup winner at any price was better than a beaten horse at long odds. Balloon King eased from 10–1 to 16s, and Soulton was next best at 20–1. There had been some more interest in Muratti, especially when it was revealed that Billy Duncan rather than Bert Morris from Tasmania would be in the saddle. At a moment when business was slow, a woman walked up to Bob Jansen and asked, 'How much money do I have to put on First Acre to win £500?'

'What's the smallest coin in your purse, madam?' the bagman asked.

'A halfpenny.'

'I'll take that! Five hundred to a halfpenny, First Acre!'

The New Zealander's odds, at least for this moment, had blown to 240,000 to one!

When it was time to move to the mounting yard, the plain-clothes police hovered in the background, while Woodcock and Phar Lap were accompanied at close quarters by two of the motor police, conspicuous in their white linen dust coats. 'Where do they think we are?' one cynic shouted out. 'Mexico? Have we all guns in our pockets?' There were a few who had grown tired of the hysteria, but most were sympathetic and saw the police protection as being part of the show.

WHEN PHAR LAP WAS still not at the course at 2.15pm, Jim Pike convinced himself that the threats had come true. He was destined never to win the Cup. Then Telford burst into the jockeys' room with his now famous red, black-and-white hooped sleeves, red cap colours, and the great dream was instantly rekindled. There was scarcely time to don the silks and Pike was on the edge of the mounting yard, watching for any sign of weakness as Woodcock gripped the bridle tight and walked the big red horse about as quickly as he dared, not wanting to over-excite him but keen, given Phar Lap had been on a motor float for more than two hours, to get his muscles loose. The topweight was now leading the parade of horses around the ring, as the 3.30pm start time grew nearer. Just a few minutes and they'd be on the track. The temptation for Telford must have been to instruct Pike to give him a rousing gallop on the way to the start, but the trainer trusted his jockey. 'See how he feels, Jim,' was all the trainer said. 'If you think he needs to stretch out, do what you think is best.'

Of course, Pike was not the only accomplished rider preparing for the race, though with Frank Dempsey replacing Ken Bracken (Poitrel's jockey in 1920, who could not get down to Soulton's handicap of 8.2) only Duncan and Nadean's rider, Alan 'Tich' Wilson, of the 1930 field had won the Cup before. Wilson had been successful in 1922 (King Ingoda) and 1923 (Bitalli). These late switches of jockeys intrigued many punters, who wondered if it had been in the plan all along. A change of rider for Spearfelt in 1926, from George Young to Hughie Cairns, had preceded a plunge that saw the five-year-old backed in from 25–1 to 10s.

Second behind Cairns in the '26 Cup was Naos, ridden by the veteran Neville Percival, who this year was on Some Quality. His gaunt, craggy features offered a marked contrast to the unlined face of Sydney-based apprentice Frank Hickey, who was nervously wearing the late John Brown's colours as he waited to mount Balloon King. Also from north of the border were Rae 'Togo' Johnstone (Star God), Ted Bartle (Tregilla), Billy Cook (Veilmond) and Stan Davidson (Donald). The last of this quartet was quite a horseman, having originally burst onto the scene by riding 34 winners in his first six months as a jockey in the Newcastle coal districts. As tough as a coal miner, he was not the sort to be messed with. One of Adelaide's strongest lightweights, 'Mick' Medhurst, had come over to ride the likely leader, Jim Scobie's second-string Temptation, while Theo Lewis (Second Wind), Harold Jones (Carradale) and Pat Tehan (Shadow King) were regulars at Flemington. The New Zealander, Turoa Webster, on First Acre, had nearly died in a race crash 12 months ago; now he had some friends in the crowd who had promised him they'd jump into the mounting yard and perform the haka if he was the first over the line.

And then there was Duncan. His Cup win had come as an 18-year-old apprentice on Night Watch in 1918, his first ride in the race, when he was so excited at the finish he forgot to stop riding until many yards past the winning post. He had also won a race on Phar Lap — the 1929 Craven Plate at Randwick — and reputedly would have been on the dual Derby winner in the Melbourne Cup four weeks after that victory had he not already accepted the ride on the Caulfield Cup winner High Syce for Jack Holt. So Duncan knew as well as anyone how good the favourite was, but unlike many he didn't see him as unbeatable. 'He's a champion horse, for sure, Mr Wren, but Manfred was better and he never won the Cup,' the jockey said to Muratti's owner as the strappers walked their horses in a circle around the mounting yard. Duncan was referring to the champion colt that won the

AJC Derby in 1925, despite being left half a furlong at the start, and then started a 7–4 favourite in that year's Cup. Amounis had been in that Derby field, but Manfred made a hack of him. Yet on the first Tuesday in November of 1925 it was Windbag that prevailed after one of Flemington's most stirring battles.

This was interesting logic, Wren thought to himself. He wasn't sure that Manfred was better than Phar Lap, and Muratti was hardly in Windbag's class. Still, he admired his jockey's optimism, and he was very happy with what he heard next. Duncan took him back to 1928, when he rode Maple in the Caulfield Cup. Jim Pike was on Gothic, the 6–4 favourite, a winner of two Newmarket Handicaps, Melbourne's top six-furlong sprint race. From the jump, Duncan sat outside Pike, keeping him in a pocket, and then took off with four furlongs to go, to make the race a true staying test. Pike's plan had been to nurse his mount for as long as possible, but with Maple three lengths clear he had to set off in pursuit. In that situation, no amount of vigorous riding could make Gothic run out a fair-dinkum mile-and-a-half.

'I'm going to try and do the same thing to Jimmy here,' Duncan said. 'If Temptation goes hard, he'll try and ride his horse quiet about fifth or sixth, I reckon. I'll sit outside him, maybe even just in front of him, and then take off at the four furlongs. If your horse is good enough, I'll either leave Phar Lap hemmed in or at the very least make him carry his weight all the way up the straight. We're a chance, I tell you.'

Wren loved the idea of Duncan riding to win. He'd run second before in the Cup, with The Rover in 1921, and didn't need to run second again. Elsewhere, conversations about riding strategies were more muted. Ned Moss listened intently as Cook was told to ride Veilmond quietly. 'He's only a little horse,' George Price said.

'He might go better with a light weight. Just make sure you get the last crack at them.' Bartle's plan was to ride Tregilla near the back, too, but then move forward about three or four furlongs from home. Mr and Mrs Battye wanted him to give the colt time to settle, but he felt it was imperative he was near Pike on the corner, from where he hoped the huge weight difference would work to his advantage. Balloon King's connections yearned for a fast pace. Harry Lewis was in a jovial mood, soaking up the thrill of having a Cup runner. 'I'm not sure she'll win as easily as she won the Australian Cup,' he told anyone who'd listen, 'but she will win.' Jim Scobie wasn't as sceptical about Carradale's chances as his owner. 'Just ride him like last year, Harry, second or third into the straight,' he said to Jones, a loyal and trusted servant. 'Medhurst will lead, if you just sit in behind him, and if the horse is in a good mood, we might surprise a few people.'

Woodcock had overheard Brophy say to Mr Telford, shortly after they arrived on the course, 'Everything's fine now.' However, as he walked Phar Lap around the mounting yard, with the trainers, owners and jockeys in their huddles and all the people looking on, he couldn't quite be sure. He was wearing his very best suit, an equally fashionable homburg, and was bursting with pride at the way good ol' Bobby paraded. Every so often, he saw a familiar face. Mr Raymond had made it (but only just he'd learn later because, unbelievably, his car broke down on the Geelong Road), so had Mr Cripps, and there were the detectives, conspicuous in their dull brown suits and matching ties among the morning suits and top hats. Then Woodcock's heart missed a beat — just for a second, he was staring eye to eye with a bloke, standing at the back of the group of reporters, who he was sure was that bastard driver of the Studebaker. Fear gave way to an anger he had never felt before, but as quickly as it appeared the face melted into the crowd. Then the trainers and jockeys were walking towards their charges. Woodcock stopped, Mr Telford legged Pike aboard, gave his champion a pat on the rump and the parade began once more.

'He looks a picture, son,' Pike said softly. 'You did a magnificent job.'

Tommy looked up at the great jockey, a man he respected so much, but he didn't say a word. He wanted to blurt out, 'He's gonna win easily, you'll see.' He also wanted to scream, 'For Christ's sake, Jim, get him down to the start quick as you can!' But he didn't. He just breathed a heavy sigh, prayed his horse was going to win, and thought of his mum, Mr Fuller, his mentor from Port Macquarie, and Mr Quinn, his first boss at Randwick. He felt a peculiar mix of pride, rage and dread. Mostly, he kept reminding himself it was almost over.

WOODCOCK MIGHT HAVE WANTED Pike to rush to the start, which was located down the end of the long straight, near where the six-furlong sprints begin, but the jockey had other plans. As topweight, No. 1, he was first out onto the turf, but while many of his rivals chose to fire up their charges by getting down to the start at fair speed, Pike was happy for Phar Lap to canter there at his own pace. The clerk of the course, on his grey steed and wearing his raincoat, was in close attendance all the way.

The final few minutes before a Melbourne Cup go by in an instant. Punters have their last-minute changes of heart, when the certainty they've been touting since Derby Day suddenly has absolutely no chance at all. The betting ring, for so long a hive of activity, is almost deserted, for even the bookmakers have left their posts to run to their preferred vantage points. In no time, the horses are at the barrier about to be called up into line, and they move in quickly, with the skilful attendants at the start fully aware that such primed equine athletes hate to be kept standing still. Only Shadow King caused any trouble in 1930, and while that volatile gelding was catching starter Rupert Greene's attention, Stan Davidson on Donald was astonished to see the black-and-white hoops on Jim Pike's right sleeve appear on his left-hand side, not Pike's left sleeve to his right.

'Hey Jim, you bastard,' Davidson cried out. 'You're supposed to be outside me.'

Pike didn't say a word, seemingly focused on keeping Phar Lap calm and still — which, as usual, was proving no easy task. The champ wanted to race. Davidson could say what he wanted; the jockeys who concerned him were Bartle, two to his left on Tregilla, little Cook, who was now right next to him on Veilmond, and Jones on Carradale, who he feared would cross over from barrier 13 and try to make life difficult. And, of course, that damn Victorian Duncan, closest to the inside rail. Pike knew that wherever he went in this race, Muratti and Duncan would be somewhere nearby. Phar Lap had originally drawn 13, from which no horse had ever won the Melbourne Cup, but he'd come in two places with the scratchings. Now he was 10 from the inside, with five horses outside him.

Davidson was about to yell out to Mr Greene or one of the attendants to set things straight when he realised Shadow King had condescended to join the line. They were now all set to go. Pike had done him again. Phar Lap stepped back, up again, threw his head about, and then Mr Greene grabbed the lever and the barrier strands shot upwards. On the Hill there was a mighty roar, one that echoed right across Australia ...

'They're off!'

CHAPTER SEVENTEEN

HERE HE COMES!

TEMPTATION WAS ONE OF the first to find grass. Getting out very, very fast also was Carradale and getting away quickly was Muratti, down on the inside, from the outside of them, Star God, which began very fast, and so did Shadow King. As they ran down to link up with the course proper, Temptation was the leader from Carradale, with moving up on the outside, Star God and Balloon King so there were three across the track, vying for the lead. Then came Muratti and First Acre, with Shadow King and Nadean next, then Tregilla, Donald, Second Wind, Soulton, Some Quality and Veilmond at the rear.

Where was the favourite? Pike had him fifth early, one off the fence, with First Acre inside him, but Balloon King and then Star God both dropped back, their jockeys desperate not to be caught wide. For about 50 yards, this was fine from Pike's perspective, as Phar Lap was directly behind Carradale, which was racing a little off the fence. But when Togo Johnstone on Star God decided to stay three wide outside the favourite, rather than drop back to midfield as young Hickey on Balloon King did, Duncan saw a chance to either push Pike wide or get him in a pocket. He booted Muratti up on the inside to second, four lengths behind the leader, which meant if Phar Lap went forward he'd be trapped outside Carradale. Instead, Pike stayed where he was, Star God on his outside, First Acre on the rail inside him, a potentially dangerous place for a short-priced favourite. The experts on the Hill were astounded Pike was riding for luck, and his legion of supporters bemoaned their misfortune as snide comments shot through the crowd that he was trapped. The doomsayers who'd predicted that some of the jockeys would ride for the bookmakers grimly shook their heads. Passing the winning post the first time, having run six furlongs and with a lap to go, Nadean raced behind Phar Lap, then Shadow King and Balloon King. Tregilla was third last, with Veilmond four lengths behind the second last horse, Some Quality.

After a fairly sharp turn left, the field ran down the straight from the mile-and-a-quarter to the mile, and the tens of thousands over on Scotchman's Hill enjoyed their best view of the race. Some, but not many, had field glasses, and it was around these experienced watchers that most had stuck, though, of course, there were experts everywhere.

'That's Phar Lap out in front,' a woman yelled. 'Good old Phar Lap. Go, you beauty!'

'That ain't Phar Lap,' a young man spat back. 'It's Temptation.'

'Are you sure? I thought that was Phar Lap's white face.'

'Phar Lap hasn't got a white face!'

By the time this small debate was resolved, the field was starting the long sweeping bend that took them from the mile to the home turn. Now all they had was a distant view of the Cup field's backsides. The young fella couldn't believe it — he'd wasted his best two furlongs of the race arguing with a lady who had no idea. He hadn't even picked out Second Wind, the horse he'd put his two shillings on, one for a win, one for a place. Maybe that was Mr Lee Steere's all red colours, back second or third last.

Many had expected Medhurst to tear away on Temptation, but instead he just loped along in front. The pace was hacking. The connections of the horses hoping for a faster race were sorely disappointed. Nightmarch's Cup had been similarly slow, something the three-year-old Phar Lap bitterly and infamously resented, but this year Pike got him to settle. There was little change in the order until passing the abattoirs at the six furlongs, when Percival made a dash on Some Quality and Bartle on Tregilla followed him. The supporters of the second favourite were on very good terms with themselves at this point, especially with Phar Lap obscured in the ruck, perhaps with nowhere to go. Veilmond moved up on the inside, and seemed to be running nicely into the race, but just as quickly he dropped back sharply, as though he'd been badly interfered with. But he'd seemed to have clear galloping room. Perhaps he'd broken down.

As they passed the four furlongs pole, Billy Duncan's instincts told him it was time to make his move. He sensed that Temptation was about to get a stitch, and to his right he saw that Jones on Carradale was feeling for the whip. If Star God could keep Pike locked in that pocket for just a little longer, or maybe Carradale might drop back on top of the favourite ... he pulled Muratti's head right, shot through the gap between Temptation and Carradale and hit the lead as they started to see the home straight.

At precisely this moment, Pike had to grab hold of Phar Lap to avoid the tiring horses that blocked his way, but Tich Wilson on Nadean didn't see the potential jam evolving in front of him, and the favourite was galloped on from behind. 'Shit, look out!' Wilson cried, while Pike was mortified. Phar Lap's head shot up as his rump went down and then, dramatically, his nose was inches from the Flemington turf, with Pike striving to maintain his seat in the saddle and his feet in the irons. Disaster seemed a stride away. It was a repeat of the Savanaka Cup — ironically, without the skulduggery. Watching in the stands through his field glasses, Telford cursed his appalling luck, while Woodcock, down in the mounting yard, could only guess from the groans of the crowd in the stands that something had happened. He'd heard someone say Phar Lap was hemmed in, but what now?

Fortunately, Pike's skill and reflexes, primed over more than 20 years as a top jockey, were fantastic. It was as if his whole career was about this moment. He reefed the gelding's head up, and then, critically, let him regain his balance and stride. For a moment they were off the bit, but still he didn't panic, and gradually that amazing cruising speed that set Phar Lap apart was revived. Only problem was, two-and-a-half furlongs to go, Duncan was away on Muratti, and Bartle on Tregilla was just a length behind him. Fortunately for Pike, Star God was struggling, a victim of his hard run out three wide the whole way. Carradale and Temptation were gone. Perhaps the horses behind him were travelling well, but the master horseman was sure that didn't matter. Not with this horse, not after all they'd been through. If he could get a clear shot at the two leaders, everything was going to be okay.

The opening appeared almost immediately. In the stands, John Wren watched Muratti sprint for about 100 yards, but past the two furlongs pole Duncan was suddenly riding for dear life. 'The damn horse is no Manfred,' Wren wryly mused to a colleague. Fifty yards further on, and Bartle, too, had gone for the whip, as the effort to race around the field to be up with the leaders quickly proved too much for Tregilla. Pike forced his way through the gap between them. 'Here he comes!' shouted his legion of supporters *en masse*, as Phar Lap quickly proved that the arduous Flemington two miles was no stumbling block. The cynics who'd underestimated him, like the now stony broke Sam Sullivan, could only cringe at their folly. Guy Raymond was savouring the realisation that his stud was now part of the Phar Lap legend, and as a racing man was revelling in the sheer joy of seeing a truly great horse in full stride. Jack Brophy wondered briefly why he'd ever thought about backing Tregilla — of course he wasn't alone in that — but what nagged at him immediately was the memory of all Phar Lap had been through. He'd seen it first hand; surely, the horse had no right to win anything after what he'd been through over the past four days, let alone dominate Australia's most important race like this?

Harry Telford was on his feet, forgetting completely he was a quiet, taciturn grouch who never showed any emotion. Woodcock could now tell by the roars of the crowd and excitement all around him that his dreams were coming true. Some men had their hats in their hands, piercing the air, yelling their hearts out as if they'd bet £500 at even money instead of five shillings. It wasn't as if they were throwing their headgear in the air — who could afford to lose a flash hat with money as tight as this? — but the mighty cheers and embrace of hugs and handshakes that took place among the members, on the Hill, the Flat, Scotchman's Hill, in pubs and offices, homes and schools, the cities and the outback, from young and old, shouted the fact this was a most famous victory. The twin realities of Phar Lap sprinting as his adversaries weakened accentuated the glorious sight of the champion bursting clear. 'Like a streak of lightning,' Pike would say afterwards. Shadow King tried to follow him through, but where once there was one length between them, now there were five. Only in the last half furlong did Pike ease off, but by then the 70th Melbourne Cup was won. The winning time was 3.27³/₄, five seconds outside the race record held by Windbag and Spearfelt, reflecting the sodden track and the slow early pace.

Behind Phar Lap, Second Wind ran the race of his life, working through the field to finish second, while it seemed Donald narrowly edged Shadow King out of third prize. First Acre was a surprise packet, finishing a fine sixth despite being stopped in his tracks in the final 10 yards, while Veilmond ran home along the inside better than anything bar the winner, before being held up by the third and fourth horses just before the post. Why had Billy Cook taken so long to make a move? Behind First Acre, there was a long gap to Tregilla, Some Quality and Soulton, and then another six lengths to the group of Muratti, Balloon King, Star God and a very weary Temptation, which staggered to the line. Nadean never recovered from the altercation with Phar Lap's hindquarters, beating only Carradale home. Mr Mackinnon's temperamental horse thus achieved the dubious distinction of finishing last in consecutive Melbourne Cups.

IT TAKES AROUND FIVE minutes for the Cup winner to 'return to scale', to come back from down by the Maribyrnong River to the gate that opens up so the champion can proudly walk back through the masses into the mounting yard. If the roars and emotion from the crowd as the field flashes past the winning post are akin to the last minute of a thrilling football grand final, when the victor returns it is as if the spectators are greeting royalty or perhaps Don Bradman returning to the dressing room after another double century. The clapping and cheering and good feeling for Phar Lap and Jim Pike were passionate and sincere. The applause began with the shouts from Scotchman's Hill as Pike pulled his favourite up, and then increased to a crescendo as the champion trotted back from the turn out of the straight, past the Hill, towards the entrance opposite the winning post. Pike had doffed his cap, his shirt was untucked at the back — could that have happened in the skirmish before the home turn? — and the two motor policemen were waiting for him, to escort him back to Telford and Woodcock. Every 10 yards or so, there were, 'Three cheers for Phar Lap!' Hats, umbrellas and winning betting tickets were held exuberantly aloft. Children tried to skip between legs, eager for one more glimpse of him.

Meanwhile, Stan Davidson could not believe that Shadow King and not his mount, Donald, had been awarded third place. While Pike was dispassionately telling Telford what an unbelievable horse Phar Lap was, Davidson was pleading, 'Is there anything we can do?' But the judge's decision was final. David Davis found himself surrounded by members of the VRC Committee, and was also being pestered by a couple of trainers wanting to confirm exactly who would be training the Cup winner in the new year. 'I dare say the horse will never be separated from Telford,' Davis said. Woodcock had a grin from ear to ear, as he rubbed Phar Lap's nose, while Ned Moss and George Price waited impatiently for Veilmond and Billy Cook. 'I think I'm going to give him a gobful,' Price snapped.

Moss was about to suggest they wait to hear what the apprentice had to say, when they looked up and saw quite clearly the imprint of a horseshoe on Cook's bloodied forehead. The poor bloke was dazed and shattered, not quite knowing what had happened to him. 'He was going easy halfway through the race,' he explained. 'Suddenly, wham! Something flies back and clouts me across the top of my nose. It nearly knocked me off the horse. I was blinded. By the time I came to, we was four lengths last. I had a dream run through in the straight until right at the finish post. Jeez, Mr Price, I'd love to know how close I would have got to the winner if I'd never got hit.'

Moss and Price were beginning to think they'd been unlucky not to win the whole thing, but then they overheard Turoa Webster talking to Pike. 'What happened to you, Jim, when your horse twisted?' the Maori asked. 'I thought you were gone for a second or two.'

The jockeys weighed in, the stewards gave the all clear (after deciding to ignore that remark about the judge cast by the rider of Donald) and immediately Pike was surrounded by reporters. First, he was asked if he thought he'd hit the front too early.

'The reason I made more use of him than I needed to,' he said politely, 'was to set up an advantage that would put the Cup beyond doubt. No flash finishes for me, no cutting it fine. It was my first Melbourne Cup win and while old Phar Lap had it in him, I wanted to put as much between me and the field as I could, so that if anything came from the clouds, it would have to be a miracle to beat me.'

Pike was usually a man of few words, but now he was caught up in the excitement. Did he have anything left at the end?

'Though I wasn't urging him past the post,' he replied, 'Phar Lap still had lots left in him and I shall never be able to tell just how much further or how much better he could have gone if he had been pressed by opposition.'

'Jim, did the fact you had to break records to win ever concern you,' asked Bert Wolfe.

'I believed the two miles with 9.12 might make a difference, thinking, "This will try you out, my lad." But look at him, Bert.

I got the shock of my life when I saw, on lifting the saddle away, that there was not the slightest sign that he had run a race. He can run two miles or any distance without getting tired.

'He is a thing of iron or steel, not flesh and blood,' Pike continued. 'He will go on indefinitely, as long as those staunch legs stand the strain. It might be two, three or more seasons. As long as he holds this spring's form, there will be nothing able to touch him in races.'

Elsewhere, Harry Telford was trying to deflect congratulations. 'Everyone has been mightily good to me,' he said. 'As I said weeks ago, those who did not want Phar Lap to run in the Cup would have had to shoot him. They probably would have succeeded in doing that only for my foreman. My thanks are due to him, and to the police and to Mr Raymond for their great help during what was, to me, a most trying period.'

Soon it was time for the presentation, where the star was Telford's four-year-old son Gerald, who some, including the trainer himself, liked to call 'Young Harry'. The diminutive lad was so natural and happy amid all the attention that he further and effectively humanised his dad. After the three-handled gold cup was presented, Telford handed it on to his young son, who was standing by his side, but Lord Somers decided to make the boy the centre of attention by lifting him up onto the small table on which the trophy had been placed prior to the ceremony. Telford junior posed cheerfully for the press photographers, but at a moment when his father was looking elsewhere he seemed on the point of losing his balance. However, before he could tumble over, Mr Mackinnon, a prim and proper chap not known for exuberance, dashed over and straightened the lad up, to the delight of onlookers. They were all one big happy family.

CHAPTER EIGHTEEN

THE PERFECT CRIME

AT THE PRECISE MOMENT the Cup presentation ended, Jack Brophy felt a hand on his shoulder, and turned to see a smiling Police Commissioner.

'I'll require a report, you understand,' Blamey said, after confirming that everything was under control.

'Yes, sir, I'll have something on your desk tomorrow,' Brophy replied.

'No, no, there's no hurry. Just get me something in due course.'

'Yes, sir.'

Half an hour later, Brophy and Saker were back in the birdcage, supervising the final act in what had been an amazing show. Woodcock and Parker were almost ready to take Phar Lap down to Boyden's float, for the drive across town to Joe Cripps' stables. There'd be no police escort. No one had requested one, or expected one. Telford had been down here earlier, and had even thrown some pound notes at the supporters who'd congregated nearby, but now he was back in the Members

Reserve, his wife and young son by his side as he chatted with David Davis and a couple of graziers from the bush who were on the lookout for a new trainer. Telford was delighted to tell them about his grand plans for 'Braeside', a new establishment he was building on a rundown property south-east of Melbourne that he had leased from the Melbourne and Metropolitan Board of Works.

After five o'clock and having failed to back the winner of the last, thus ensuring a losing day on the punt, Brophy and Saker were walking to their car when they spotted a newsboy by his stand, yelling, 'Piper!... Piper!... Get your Cup Day 'Erald!... Piper!' The senior detective pulled a penny and a halfpenny from his pocket. It was about all he had left.

The main headline, bold from one side of the front page to the other, read 'HOW PHAR LAP WON THE MELBOURNE CUP'. Gwyn Jones' story about how the gelding had the race won 'all the way' was splashed over four-and-a-half columns. There were quotes from Telford and the jockeys. And there was a story about 'Phar Lap's Hiding Place' that avoided any mention at all of why such subterfuge had been deemed necessary. There was more Cup coverage on the inside pages, astonishingly extensive given that the trophy had been handed over less than two hours earlier. However, there was nothing, it seemed, on what had four days earlier been seen as a most heinous crime.

'No, hang on, Harold, you have got your name in here,' Brophy said.

On page three, down the bottom of column two, were four sentences ...

Detective Saker, who is investigating the attempt to shoot Phar Lap at Caulfield on Saturday, has ascertained that the numbers on the car used by the men involved in the shooting were both fictitious.

One number was cancelled some time ago by the motor registration branch, and the other was issued to a footballer.

Though no clue as to the identity of the men who fired the shot had been obtained, Saker is still hopeful of tracing the car.

At present he is concentrating on a search for a car which was seen in the Caulfield district some time after the shooting.'

If Brophy had looked more closely, he would have also seen these few lines halfway through a separate report on page three. There was that word 'dastardly' again ...

The Chicago touch given to the Cup by the discharge of a shotgun at Phar Lap, the hot favourite, provided a sensational topic before the racing business of the day began. Such a dastardly attempt added weight to the idolatry heaped upon the champion ...

That, in the end, became the essence of the story. Rather than stopping Phar Lap, the 'shooting' enhanced the legend — of the horse and the Cup. It was, in a sense, the perfect crime. Nobody got hurt or caught, and by the end of Melbourne Cup 1930 every single person involved, perpetrators and victims, seemed better off. Sure, one mighty horse and some innocent individuals had been cruelly frightened, but Phar Lap was now considered in many people's eyes to be better even than Carbine (there is no higher praise), and Tommy Woodcock was the courageous horseman who saved him. Harry Telford was not only rich, he'd reclaimed his reputation that had been so tarnished by the late scratching from the Caulfield Cup, and he was confirmed as Phar

Lap's long-term trainer, too. David Davis, Eric Connolly and Maude Vandenburg had collected on their double, however big or small their final profit was. Guy Raymond had gained priceless exposure for St Albans and was the darling of the VRC Committee (an opening had come up among this elite group and Mr Mackinnon had assured him he was the prime candidate). Raymond had also taken a liking to Stan Boyden, suggesting that, yes, there would definitely be opportunities at the stud if that was what Boyden wanted. Bobby Parker was a trusted apprentice in one of Australia's fastest-growing stables, with ambitions to be like Jim Pike, who had just crowned his much-acclaimed career by winning the Melbourne Cup.

The race itself was even further entrenched in the national consciousness. With the wireless now reaching almost every ear in the country, nearly every Australian alive in 1930 would remember where they were when Phar Lap won the Cup. Jack Brophy and Harold Saker certainly would. The past four days had not done either detective any harm. Brophy was sure his popularity with Commissioner Blamey had risen, though privately he conceded that probably had more to do with the summons he delivered to the Police Association secretary than because of the way he handled the Phar Lap case. Whatever, his chances of one day becoming CIB chief had definitely improved. Saker was happy with the manner in which he'd used his contacts in the racing industry, never betraying a trust. Maybe one day he'd end up a steward, or something like that. There'd be worse jobs.

The people behind the gun and the wheel of the Studebaker had only one problem: they couldn't tell anyone how clever they'd been. To do so would risk the wrath of both their employers and the police force, at a time when they could ill afford to be searching for work or a criminal lawyer. Looking for employment of some kind was what poor Sam Sullivan would soon be doing. He was one person who didn't gain out of the Phar Lap shooting, but then he didn't have anything to do with it. There was no chance Sullivan would be at the Victorian Club for settling tomorrow; the best he could hope for was understanding and time, two things big punters rarely had. But he wouldn't do a bolt, he was bigger than that. At least he was wiser. You never underestimate a true champion

The papers themselves couldn't complain. Lord Northcliffe, one of the great pioneers of the British newspaper industry, had adopted Keith Murdoch as something of a protégé when the Australian had been in London during the War. In a letter written to Murdoch not long after he took over as the *Herald's* Editor-in-Chief in 1921, Northcliffe advised:

> The *Herald* has a very bad name in Australia, and not only in Melbourne. I have never heard one word in its favour ... you have got to live down a past. When you have done that, and some big news happens to come along, you will get all the new readers you want.

Keith Murdoch never lost sight of the value of 'big news'. It first worked for him with the Gun Alley murder, the ghastly crime story that made his paper's name. His critics saw this new approach as 'sensationalism'; most agreed he made the *Herald* a more interesting and influential newspaper. It certainly sold more copies. His aggressive methods also made the newspaper game in Melbourne much more competitive. In the case of the 1930 Cup, there is no indication at all that Murdoch was personally involved in the plot to 'shoot' Phar Lap. On the contrary, he was undoubtedly a man above that sort of thing. However, the philosophy he brought to the Australian newspaper business might well have been a factor — whether the reporters involved (from his own staff or from rival papers) were trying to create the news or have some fun with the fact that a racehorse was dominating the news. For four days following the attack at the corner of James and Etna Streets, the Cup favourite, his well-being and his whereabouts was the biggest tale in town. Bluey the dog was bigger than Bradman. In normal circumstances, the story of the shooting would have stayed on or near the front page for a week or more. But these were not normal circumstances.

Finally, there were all the punters, big and small, who picked up good money in lean times. If all the people who claimed they took the double really did, the bookies would have owed about three million quid, but without doubt there were many winners from all over the country. They mightn't have sent the bookies broke, but they did them no favours. Provincial papers in every state and territory ran stories of locals who'd struck gold, and one leading Melbourne bookie revealed he was writing cheques to be sent as far afield as Derby in Western Australia and Townsville in Queensland. Meanwhile, a telegram was coming east from Perth, sent by a group of punters who'd taken the Amounis–Phar Lap double soon after weights had been released back at the start of July. Eric Connolly might not have got long odds about the double, but these blokes certainly did. Their cable read:

Phar Lap, c/- H. Telford, Melbourne — If you could only stand on your hind legs and talk, we'd make you Prime Minister of Australia.

MELBOURNE CUP 1930

Run November 4; Two miles; Race started at 3.31pm

Position	Name	Trainer	Jockey	Weight	Age	Barrier
1	**Phar Lap**	HR Telford	J Pike	9.12	4	11
2	**Second Wind**	J Holt	T Lewis	8.12	5	2
3	**Shadow King**	E Fisher	P Tehan	8.4	5	7
4	**Donald**	EF Smith	S Davidson	8.12	9	10
5	**Veilmond**	G Price	W Cook	7.7	3	9
6	**First Acre**	AD Webster	T Webster	7.11	8	4
7	**Tregilla**	CO Battye	E Bartle	7.9	3	8
8	**Soulton**	L Robertson	F Dempsey	8.2	6	5
9	**Some Quality**	WJ Nolan	N Percival	7.11	6	6
10	**Balloon King**	RD O'Donnell	F Hickey	7.6	3	14
11	**Muratti**	F Musgrave	W Duncan	7.6	7	1
12	**Star God**	C O'Rourke	WR Johnstone	7.11	6	15
13	**Temptation**	J Scobie	R Medhurst	7.0	5	3
14	**Nadean**	WN Brodie	A Wilson	8.0	6	12
15	**Carradale**	J Scobie	H Jones	8.9	4	13

Won by three lengths, ¾ length; Time: 3.27¾; Attendance: 72,358; Stakes: £12,429
(First: £9429, including Cup valued at £200; Second: £2000, Third: £1000)

Market

8–11	Phar Lap
5	Tregilla
16	Balloon King
20	Nadean, Soulton
25	Carradale, Muratti, Veilmond
40	Star God
50	Second Wind, Shadow King, Some Quality, Temptation
66	Donald
100	First Acre

Scratchings

John Buchan, Walpilly

Notes

- 'Position' indicates finishing position
- The weights are in stones and pounds. Thus '9.12' is nine stone, 12 pound. By way of comparison with modern weights and measures, one kilogram is equivalent to two pound, three ounces; 9.12 equals 62.65kg.
- 'Barrier' indicates the starting position for each horse, after the two scratchings.

POSTSCRIPT

Following the 1930 Melbourne Cup, a correspondent from the *Sydney Sportsman* wrote:

> General opinion among Sydney trainers is that Phar Lap passed a cold motor car just as it happened to be moving off in the early hours and the noise of the exhaust was construed as a shot of a gun ...

There was some justification for this cynicism, given that the initial reports out of Melbourne indicated there was no evidence of a shot having been fired. The *Sydney Truth*, published on the Sunday morning, made a great deal of the unexplained lack of damage that might be expected from the discharge of a shotgun.

Because of time constraints, many country newspapers — including the *Geelong Advertiser*, the *Ballarat Courier* and Albury–Wodonga's *Border Morning Mail* — carried a wire story filed on the Saturday night in their Monday morning editions. When this report, which seems entirely credible, was written, the pellets were still to be discovered. It read in part:

> The Glenhuntly police were informed and they communicated with the Criminal Investigation Branch. Detective Harold Saker was rushed to the scene of the shooting and made investigations. He was unable, however, to find any trace of the car or its occupants. Neither were there any marks which might have been caused by bullets or shotgun pellets ...

It seems astonishing that an officer of the ability and experience of Saker was unable on the Saturday to find the pellets and shot marks that were discovered the following day. The trainer Joe Bird was able to find a cardboard wad on the Saturday, but could also not find any pellets or any marks where pellets had struck the fence. This is the essence of the mystery.

For our earlier book, *Phar Lap* (Allen & Unwin, Sydney, 2000), Senior Constable Ray Vincent, a ballistics expert from the Victorian Forensic Centre, informed us that a shotgun firing a cartridge of No. 6 pellets at a fence from 20 metres will leave an elliptical shot pattern approximately 50 centimetres wide in its narrowest dimension. And it will leave 270 to 300 pellets in the fence. This was confirmed in a subsequent discussion with Bill Shelton from the Sporting Shooters' Association of Australia, who also explained that No. 6 pellets fired from 20 metres would not seriously hurt a horse. The best chance of causing major damage in such circumstances might be through a wound subsequently getting infected. No. 6 pellets are more appropriate for trying to kill ducks than for maiming thoroughbreds.

It was the *Argus* that reported that No. 6 pellets were found at the scene. Interestingly, though, in Jack Brophy and Harold Saker's final report on the Phar Lap case, written on December 1, 1930, the detectives contend that it was heavier No. 4 pellets that were discovered. This is one of a number of areas in which their summation differs from the press reports of a month earlier. 'On the 2nd November a close inspection of the spot where the shooting occurred was made by us,' the policemen wrote in their report, 'and several shot pellets (No. 4) were found.'

(Brophy and Saker's report is one of the eight documents that remain in the police file of the case, which is currently held by the Public Records Office Victoria [VPRS 807/PO]. The others are

Saker's report of November 1 [see pages 84–85 of this book], David Davis' posting of a £100 reward, a 'telephone message' and two handwritten notes relating to the car registration number provided by Woodcock, a report by Senior Constable Davis, written on November 2, which summarises his initial findings, and the 'crank' warning letter [and its envelope] that was written on *Herald* newsprint [see pages 138–139]. Any other official documentation relating to the case appears to have been lost or destroyed.)

In their December 1 report, Brophy and Saker also contradict the press when it comes to the question of damage caused to the fence. 'A large number of shot marks were clearly shown on the pickets of the fence,' the detectives wrote. 'These facts indicate that the shot fired was not a blank.' If this was true, it is extremely surprising that there was no mention of a *large number* of pellets being in the fence in any of the published newspaper reports. It was not like the journalists covering the case to be cautious. The *Age* reporter was able to count the individual pellet marks on one hand, while the *Herald* featured a photograph of just two pellet marks, a centimetre or two apart.

Brophy and Saker's report ends this way:

Certain information has been received by us regarding who is suspected of the offence but owing to the fact that we have no identification our enquiries have been hampered.

This matter will be further followed up and in the event of anything tangible coming to hand action will immediately be taken.

This is their last word on the subject. The report was sent to the Chief Commissioner's office. General Blamey saw it, was happy with it, signed it, and that was end of the matter.

Brophy and Saker's report might be riddled with contradictions; or it might be a masterly piece of craftsmanship. No one reading it can be of any view other than that the official police verdict is that a cartridge of potentially lethal shot was discharged in a suburban street — in the direction of a great racehorse, the Melbourne Cup favourite, and his strapper. A serious crime has been committed, the report states, and we know who did it. If anyone was inclined to claim ownership of a prank, reading this report would ensure their silence.

Since Cup Day, no new evidence had been found. No one was ever charged. In the years since that final report was written, a number of people have claimed to know who the offenders were, and always the accused have been 'bookmakers' or evil people 'working for bookmakers'. However, no individual has ever been named. No one has ever claimed responsibility.

In 1932 an article about Phar Lap's attempt on the 1931 Melbourne Cup was printed in *The Bloodstock Breeders' Review*, a conservative publication from the United Kingdom. It contained the following:

In the story we wrote about last year's Melbourne Cup, mention is made of the report that, early in the morning of the day Phar Lap won the Melbourne Stakes a shot was fired at him (without effect) while he was returning to his stable from the training ground at Caulfield. The news created a tremendous sensation. It was stated that the man with the gun was in a motor car 'which disappeared from the scene of the outrage at top speed, and the miscreant was not discovered'. And no wonder, for according to a letter we have received from a friend well known in Melbourne press circles, 'The story was jokingly concocted by three journalists on the Thursday before Derby Day.'

We gather that the conspiring journalists were animated by an irresistible desire to make fun of the 'Phar Lap hysteria' with which Australians have been afflicted.

This is arguably the best explanation ever put forward for what happened at the corner of James and Etna Streets on the morning of Derby Day 1930. Perhaps adding weight to this unknown correspondent's claim is the fact that the crank letter — the one addressed to 'Det. Sgt. Piggot' from 'One that Knows', which was written on the back of the sheet of ripped newsprint and which we featured on pages 137–139 — remains in the police file. That piece of paper had on the other side of it, in big red letters, the 'A', 'L' and 'D' of the word 'HERALD'. Why was this one warning letter filed for posterity? It might not have been beyond Jack Brophy to leave such a clue. As Kevin Morgan documents in his book *Gun Alley: Murder, Lies and Failure of Justice* (Simon & Schuster, Sydney, 2005), when researchers into the Gun Alley murder gained access to the official police file many years after the event, they found material that normally would have been destroyed when the case was closed. Instead, it was as if the evidence had been left for a future generation to reinterpret — evidence that might have cleared Colin Ross, the man who had been executed for the crime.

It is supposition on our part when we suggest that the police went to the newspaper chiefs, who then issued a firm directive for the story to be quashed and for those responsible to keep quiet about it. However, this seems as rational as any explanation for the fact that the incident simply disappeared from the news pages. Over the weekend, the attack on the Cup favourite had been the biggest news story in town, but by Tuesday it was scarcely being referred to and by Wednesday there were no reports specifically about the affair to be found in any of the daily Melbourne newspapers. The sole exception to this was a brief yarn on page eight of the *Sun News-Pictorial* of Thursday, November 6, which reduced what might have been an attempted murder to farce:

London, Wednesday: Tom Webster, in a cartoon in the *Daily Mail*, depicts Phar Lap's amazement when the shooting began. The cartoon suggests Phar Lap must have thought he was living in Chicago, and refused, like a good gangster, to name his assailants.

Webster depicts the Australian jockey of the future, armour-clad, getting instructions from the owner in a big-gunned one-man tank with the horses going to the post for the Melbourne Cup inside tanks equipped with machine guns.

Almost certainly, Jack Brophy and Harold Saker knew more about the Phar Lap 'shooting' than they were prepared to officially report. With police resources and political tensions being what they were in 1930, they may well have decided that their efforts were better spent elsewhere than trying to nail the perpetrator of a prank. The best way to solve this crime was to let the legend live, and to kill the story.

HOW BADLY WERE THE bookmakers hurt by Phar Lap's win in the 1930 Melbourne Cup? One newspaper report published a couple of days before the race suggested that bookies were facing payouts of £500,000. However, another story claimed that a Carradale win would be their worst result. For every report published after the Cup that stated that the bookmakers had been wiped out, another said there had been worse years.

Of course, there were many stories of punters collecting significant wins, but this was only natural given that Amounis and Phar Lap were always popular with punters betting on the two Cups. Most likely, it was a bad result for the bookmakers, but not the worst; a number of bookies were hit hard, but only one or two were devastated. The Melbourne *Truth* reported that one prominent bagman (whom it did not name) was unable to meet his obligations, and there was an amusing story in a couple of papers about another bookmaker who was required for jury duty on the Wednesday after the Cup. He was excused, on the grounds that he needed time to settle his bets.

Perhaps the best guide as to how hard the Melbourne bookmakers were hit comes from the minute books of the VRC Committee. In the months after the Cup, only four bookmakers — one from the Rails, two from the Hill and one from the Flat — had their licences revoked because they could not meet their liabilities. Given the state of the Australian economy at the time and the generally hazardous nature of the bookmaking business, this doesn't seem too many. It is impossible to confirm that any of these insolvencies came about solely because of Phar Lap's win. In the same period, the VRC Secretary noted more instances of punters not being able to honour bets than bookies having inadequate funds in their bags.

This is why we created the character of bookmaker Sam Sullivan — he is the only major fictional character in *Melbourne Cup 1930*. It would have been wrong for us to try to pin the crime on a real-life bookmaker, even one or more of the men named in the VRC Committee's minute book.

THE VRC HANDICAPPER GAVE *Phar Lap* 10.10 for the 1931 Melbourne Cup, which meant he would have smashed Carbine's weight-carrying record had he won. However, he finished eighth as a 3-1 favourite. It was the first time the champion had started at odds that generous since September 1929, and the first time since February 1930 he'd finished worse than second in a race. By Cup Day 1931, Phar Lap was a tired horse. Soon after, however, he was on a boat to New Zealand, on to California, and then down the long road to the Agua Caliente racetrack situated just on the southern side of the US–Mexican border. There, in the rich Agua Caliente Handicap, Phar Lap produced one of his greatest performances, sitting four or five wide until he took off five furlongs from home to win by two lengths. That one win was enough for some US racing historians to rate Phar Lap one of the greatest horses to race in North America.

Sixteen days later Phar Lap was dead, in what many thought to be sinister circumstances. The cause of his death remained inexplicable until 2000, when in *Phar Lap* we asserted — after consulting a number of respected veterinary surgeons — that the 1930 Melbourne Cup winner was attacked by an enterotoxin of bacterial origin, a poison, that caused Anterior Enteritis (or more correctly Duodenitis–Proximal jejunitis). This disease syndrome was not identified in the veterinary science literature until the early 1980s, so it was never considered as a possible cause of Phar Lap's death. In the five years since our book was published, no one has refuted this explanation.

Phar Lap died with his head cradled in the arms of his great mate, *Tommy Woodcock*, who had become the champion's trainer when Harry Telford opted not to go to North America. Returning to Australia, Woodcock became a mentor to a number of outstanding apprentices and something of a 'battling' trainer until 1977, when his tough stayer Reckless won the Sydney, Adelaide and Brisbane Cups before running second to Gold And Black in the Melbourne Cup. Tommy Woodcock died in 1985.

Jim Pike was one man who never lost sight of Woodcock's

contribution to Phar Lap's extraordinary success. After the 1930 Melbourne Cup, Pike gave the strapper £200, part as a token of his own appreciation, part because he knew Harry Telford had not been generous in rewarding his foreman for all that he'd been through to get Phar Lap to the Cup. The great jockey should have won a second Melbourne Cup in 1934, but a suspension cost him the ride on Peter Pan. Soon after, his constant weight battles finally beat him, and he retired from the saddle. Jim Pike died in 1969.

John O'Connell Brophy's career progressed quite nicely for most of the five-and-a-half years after Phar Lap's Melbourne Cup. Late in 1930 he and Commissioner Blamey got their man when Victor Price, the secretary of the Victorian Police Association, was sentenced to one month's imprisonment (reduced to a £10 fine on appeal) for counselling disobedience of an order of the Chief Commissioner. However, they couldn't break the association, which survives to this day. On May 2, 1936, Brophy became head of the CIB, but within three weeks everything went terribly wrong. On the night of May 22, at Royal Park in Melbourne, Brophy was seriously wounded when shot three times while sitting in a chauffeur-driven car. Two women were also in the vehicle. Ludicrously, the first report out of the Chief Commissioner's office stated that the CIB Chief had shot himself; the second version of events was that Brophy had been shot by unknown villains after going to the park to meet an informer. No mention was made of the women. Brophy's career was effectively ruined, as was Blamey's police career after a Royal Commission into the affair found the Commissioner had been less than truthful when providing various accounts of what might have gone on. Despite this, Blamey went on to lead the Australian forces in World War II and in 1950 become the first Australian-born Field Marshal. Jack Brophy left the police force in 1937, ruled medically unfit, and died in 1946.

Harold Saker remained in the Victoria Police Force until 1938, when he resigned to become the VRC's 'Racecourse Inspector'. This role was described in the VRC's official history, *A Century Galloped By*, as being 'to carry out investigations to assist stewards, enquire, as required, into the activities of people licensed by the VRC and to have the right to remove undesirables from Flemington and other Victorian racecourses'. Later, Saker became a stipendiary steward, in charge of country racing. After his first wife died, he remarried (with the legendary racecaller Bert Bryant as his best man) — at the age of 83!

Guy Raymond succeeded in his ambition to restore St Albans Stud to its former glory. Among the horses bred there were the great mare Tranquil Star, a winner of 23 races including two Cox Plates and a Caulfield Cup, and two Melbourne Cup winners — Sirius (1944) and Rimfire (1948). Rimfire was trained by Stan Boyden, Phar Lap's float driver in 1930. Raymond had been elected to the VRC Committee in 1931 (where he was joined in 1947 by General Blamey) and served with great distinction, perhaps his most notable achievement being to lead the move to establish an apprentices' school.

Harry Telford, the man who discovered the only horse to become a genuine Australian icon, preferred to stay at his 'Braeside' property with what had become a large stable of horses, rather than travel with the champion to North America for the Agua Caliente Handicap. Telford spent heavily on well-bred yearlings, but future triumphs eluded him — his only big-race victory after 1932 coming in 1953, when Silver Hawk won the Rosehill Guineas at 100-1. Observers noted that Silver Hawk was easily the tallest horse in the race, at least 17 hands, but he never won another race. Harry Telford died in September 1960, almost penniless, knowing better than anyone that there will never be another Phar Lap.

NOTES AND SOURCES

General Notes

Newspapers, periodicals and magazines consulted during the writing of *Melbourne Cup 1930* include: *The Advertiser* (Adelaide), *The Age* (Melbourne), *The Argus* (Melbourne), *The Arrow* (Sydney), *The Australasian* (Melbourne), *The Ballarat Courier* (Ballarat), *The Bloodstock Breeders' Review* (London), *The Border Morning Mail* (Albury–Wodonga), *Daily Telegraph* (Sydney), *The Geelong Advertiser* (Geelong), *The Herald* (Melbourne), *Labor Daily* (Sydney), *The Leader* (Melbourne), *The Referee* (Sydney), *The Register* (Adelaide), *Smith's Weekly* (Sydney), *The Sporting Globe* (Melbourne), *The Sporting Judge* (Melbourne), *The Sun* (Sydney), *The Sun News–Pictorial* (Melbourne), *The Sydney Morning Herald* (Sydney), *The Sydney Sportsman* (Sydney), *Truth* (Melbourne), *Truth* (Sydney), *Turf Monthly* (Sydney), *The Wagga Advertiser* (Wagga Wagga).

Most of the conversations between major characters recounted in *Melbourne Cup 1930* came from our own speculations. The stories of past Melbourne Cups have all been documented, and came from a wide range of sources — most notably from Bill Ahern's superb *A Century of Winners: The Saga of 121 Melbourne Cups* (Boolarong Publications, Brisbane 1982) and Maurice Cavanough's *The Melbourne Cup 1861–1982* (Currey O'Neil, Melbourne 1983).

For stories of Australian gamblers such as Eric Connolly, Billy Tindall, Maude Vandenburg and Andy Kerr, David Hickie's *Gentleman of the Australian Turf* (Angus & Robertson, Sydney 1986) was extremely helpful, as were Clive Inglis' two books from the 1950s, *Horsesense* (published in 1950) and *More Horsesense* (1959). Inglis' books were especially useful in providing information on Ned Moss, John Brown, Frank Shillabeer and the Call of the Card.

For information on the history of St Albans Stud, we consulted Robert Windmill's *Geelong Racing: The History of Horse Racing in Geelong* (Robert Windmill, Newtown 1988). For Phar Lap's time at the stud in November 1930, Cavanough's *The Melbourne Cup 1861–1982*, Isabel Carter's *Phar Lap: The Story of the Big Horse* (Lansdowne Press, Melbourne

1964), and the Melbourne *Truth* of November 8, 1930, were very helpful.

For Thomas Blamey, we consulted David Horner's *Blamey: The Commander-in-Chief* (Allen & Unwin, Sydney 1998), Michael Cathcart's *Defending the National Tuckshop* (McPhee Gribble/Penguin, Melbourne 1988) and the *Australian Defence Force Journal* for May/June 2001.

For Keith Murdoch, we consulted *Keith Murdoch: Founder of a Media Empire*, by RM Younger (HarperCollins, Sydney 2003), *In Search of Keith Murdoch* by Desmond Zwar (Macmillan, South Melbourne 1980) and William Shawcross' *Rupert Murdoch* (Random House, Sydney 1997).

For John O'Connell Brophy, *Crimes That Shocked Australia* by Alan Sharpe (The Currawong Press, Sydney 1982), Kevin Morgan's *Gun Alley: Murder, Lies and Failure of Justice* (Simon & Schuster, Sydney 2005) and *Famous Australasian Crimes* by Tom Gurr and HH Cox (Shakespeare Head Press, London 1957) proved interesting.

Much of the biographical material for Phar Lap, Harry Telford, Tommy Woodcock and Jim Pike came from our book *Phar Lap* (Allen & Unwin, Sydney 2000)

Notes Relating to Specific Pages
In the preface (page vii) we state that the origins of Phar Lap's name were Siamese. Some historians have suggested that the name came from another Asian language, but in the 1932 film, *The Mighty Conqueror*, Harry Telford stated that 'Phar Lap' was Siamese for 'sky blink' or 'lightning'.

In Senior Constable John Davis' November 2 report of the Phar Lap 'shooting', held by the Public Records Office Victoria, he stated that Tommy Woodcock memorised the *back* number plate and that James Creed noted the *front* plate (see pages 3, 10, 13 and 44 of this book). This was the reverse of what had been reported in the *Herald*. In all instances where Davis' report and the *Herald* story disagree, we accepted the version of events provided by Davis, a man with 25 years experience as a front-line police officer.

The story of The Hon. Thomas Reibey and the 1882 Cup (page 22) came from the *Referee* of October 20, 1913. For the story of 'Patrona' (page 23), see the *Referee*, October 29, 1930.

A 1930 Cup doubles betting card dated September 23, which has Amounis–Phar Lap as a 'special' at 20–1 (page 31), is on display at Museum Victoria's Phar Lap exhibit.

The *Herald* story quoted on pages 38–40 appeared in the 'Last Race Final Sports' evening edition. Parts of this story may not have been in earlier editions, so some licence is used when we have Jack Brophy reading the entire story just after 2pm (page 41).

The tale of Harold Saker and Squizzy Taylor (pages 41–42) was adapted from a story in *The Bert Bryant Story*, by Bert Bryant with Neill Phillipson (Rigby, Melbourne 1979).

The story of Harry Telford receiving a phone threat not long after the 'shooting' (page 44) was told by Jim Pike in the Sydney *Daily Telegraph*, March 26, 1936. The tale of Pike being approached by Mick Polson before the 1930 Cup (page 87) came from Bill Whittaker's story 'Devoted to the Cause', which appeared in our book, *Phar Lap*. The story of Pike, Phar Lap and Woodcock (page 93) came from another Pike article for the *Telegraph*, April 21, 1936.

Tommy Woodcock's explanation of 'strapping' and memories of his early life (pages 89–91) were sourced from Jan Wositzky's *Tommy Woodcock 1905–1985* (Greenhouse Publications, Melbourne 1986). Wositzky's book was also helpful in regards to Phar Lap's journey to St Albans and his time at the stud.

Much of the information about the two number plates on page 103 came from the official police file. However, the link between a 'footballer' and the number noted by James Creed was only reported in the press, who were quoting Harold Saker. That footballer was never identified, so we created 'Ted Trudgett'.

The tale of Don Bradman being 'caught napping' (page 108) was adapted from a brief story that appeared in the Adelaide *Register* of November 3, 1930.

Bert Wolfe's tale of Lord Cardigan's Cup win (page 111–112) came from one of a series of articles Wolfe wrote for the *Herald* in Cup week 1960. The story of the unsuccessful 'Savanaka coup' (page 112–114) was adapted from the press reports of the day, Cavanough's *The Melbourne Cup 1861–1982*, Hickie's *Gentleman of the Australian Turf*, and the *Leader* of November 5, 1921. The story of Bravo's Cup and the role played by Mr AP Morris (page 115) came from that *Leader* article.

The comments of Harry Telford (page 120) appeared in the *Sun News-Pictorial* for November 3, 1930.

The *Victorian Police Journal* for 1930 provided much of the information concerning General Blamey's dispute with the Victorian Police Association (pages 126–127). The discussion between Harry Alderman and General Blamey (page 139) came from Jack Gallaway's *Blamey and Macarthur at War* (UQP, Brisbane, 2000).

James Wilson junior (page 153) was interviewed by the *Sun News-Pictorial* at Flemington on Cup Day 1930. The potential sweepstakes wins of Archie Campbell and Alick Homewood (page 172) were featured in most of the daily newspapers on the morning of the 1930 Cup.

The bet taken on Cup Day by Bob Jansen of £5000 to £4000 about Phar Lap (page 174) was reported, though the punter was not identified. The bet of £500 to a halfpenny about First Acre (page 182) was noted by the Sydney *Sun* of November 5, but was not attributed to Jansen.

The Cup-eve meeting between Harry Telford and VRC Secretary Arthur Kewney (page 175) was reported by the Sydney *Sun* of November 3.

The comments made by patrons in the birdcage on Cup Day (page 181), comparing Phar Lap to Carbine and Poseidon, were reported in the *Age* of November 5.

For Billy Duncan (page 184–186), we consulted DL Bernstein's *First Tuesday in November: The Story of the Melbourne Cup* (William Heinemann Ltd, Melbourne 1969) and Maurice Cavanough's *The Caulfield Cup* (Jack Pollard Pty Ltd, Sydney 1976).

The start of chapter 17 (page 189) is something of a small tribute to Bert Bryant. When Geoff Armstrong was a boy, his dad taped Bryant's call of Silver Knight's Cup of (1971) — and that cassette was then played over and over, like most kids do with music, until every word was memorised. Armstrong can still hear Bert Bryant beginning: *Sandsequin was one of the first to find grass. Getting out very, very fast also was Skint Dip and getting away quickly was Lincoln's Inn, down on the inside, from the outside of them, Gnapur, which began very fast and so did Fair Sample ...*

The debate between two spectators on Scotchman's Hill (page 190) was adapted from the *Age*'s description of Cup Day at that venue, which appeared on November 5, 1930.

The story of Phar Lap nearly falling in the Cup (page 192) was adapted from an article by Bill Priestly ('Musket') that appeared in the *Sporting Globe*, November 12, 1930.

The slow-motion film of the 1930 Cup finish (see *Phar Lap: The People's Champion*; Raceplay 1999) shows that Donald might have finished third in the 1930 Cup (page 195). The *Referee* of November 5, 1930, reported: 'The Sydney horse who ran well was Donald and his failure to get third prize caused some discussion. It was thought he had just dashed up in the last stride to beat Shadow King for that position. As the press box overlooks the judge's box and most of the occupants were agreed that he was third and Shadow King fourth, it can well be imagined that the tussle was close.' Shadow King went on to become one of the Cup's most enduring figures, running second in 1931, third in 1932, second again in 1933 and fourth as a 10-year-old in 1935.

Billy Cook's post-race revelations (page 195) came from Bernstein's *First Tuesday in November*. David Davis' comments about Harry Telford continuing to train Phar Lap after the Cup (also page 195) appeared in most of the daily papers for November 5, 1930. Jim Pike's comments (pages 196–197) were adapted from the *Referee*, November 26, 1930. Harry Telford's son Gerald (page 197) was referred to as 'Harry' in newspaper reports of the Cup presentation and in post-race quotes attributed to Telford.

Lord Northcliffe's letter to Keith Murdoch (page 202) is part of the 'Papers of Keith Arthur Murdoch (1886–1952)' collection held by the National Library of Australia.

The sending of the telegram by a syndicate of Western Australian punters (page 203) was reported in the *Border Morning Mail* of November 10, 1930.

Other books consulted during the writing of *Melbourne Cup 1930* were: Les Carlyon, *Gallipoli* (Pan Macmillan, Sydney 2001); James Griffin, *John Wren: A Life Considered* (Scribe Publications, Melbourne 2004); and John Pancini, *A Century Galloped By: The First 100 Years of the Victoria Racing Club* (Victoria Racing Club, Melbourne 1988).

ACKNOWLEDGEMENTS

The authors are extremely grateful to the many people who supported this book, especially Sue Hines, Clare Emery and all the good people at Allen & Unwin.

Special thanks to:

- Steve Eather from the Victoria Police Museum, for his help with all our questions concerning Jack Brophy, Harold Saker and police operations in the 1930s.
- The staff at the Public Record Office Victoria, the Victoria Police Historical Unit, the NSW and Victorian State Libraries, the National Library of Australia and the Footscray Historical Society.
- Anne Ryan from the Victorian Police Association, who gave us access to the Association's archives and especially to the *Victorian Police Journal* for 1930.
- Peter Remfrey from the NSW Police Association.
- Kathy Peters and Joe McGrath from the VRC.
- Bill Shelton and Michael Gill from the Sporting Shooters' Association of Australia.
- The people responsible for the Australian War Memorial's website, which is fantastic.

Thanks also to Bill Charles, Bart Cummings, Ian Heads, Phillip Jennings, Ali Orman, Murray Lembit, Ralph Stavely and Larry Writer, who answered questions and offered support at various stages of the project. And to Graeme 'the Legend' Jones, Anne Reilly and the 'Queen of Commas', Sarah Shrubb, for helping to make the book a reality.